Acting for Beginners

A Heart-centered Approach to Acting

(The Beginner's Guide to Becoming an Actor and Getting That First Role)

Marcie Griffin

Published By **Chris David**

Marcie Griffin

Acting for Beginners: A Heart-centered Approach to Acting (The Beginner's Guide to Becoming an Actor and Getting That First Role)

ISBN 978-1-998769-59-9

No part of this guidebook shall be reproduced in any form without permission in writing from the publisher except in the case of brief quotations embodied in critical articles or reviews.

Legal & Disclaimer

The information contained in this ebook is not designed to replace or take the place of any form of medicine or professional medical advice. The information in this ebook has been provided for educational & entertainment purposes only.

The information contained in this book has been compiled from sources deemed reliable, and it is accurate to the best of the Author's knowledge; however, the Author cannot guarantee its accuracy and validity and cannot be held liable for any errors or omissions. Changes are periodically made to this book. You must consult your doctor or get professional medical advice before using any of the suggested remedies, techniques, or information in this book.

Table of contents

Chapter 1: Being From Your Curb Zone

Drama classes are designed to help actors find their inner zone. From this place, they can easily transform into new characters. It is however difficult to sustain this level of focus.

The truth lies beneath all the masks and fears we use to hide our insecurities and fears. This is the ultimate quest in life. This manual is a method that will help you focus your mental eyes so that you become a clear actor. It's like being a child.

LESSON 1.

PSYCHIC METHODOLOGY

As a psychic-level actor you can expand your intellect and emotional range until you are able, during rehearsals, to instantly convert each scene into visual or emotional impulses that are stored in your subconscious data bank. The actual reading is as easy as repeating the words. All the appropriate images and emotions are automatically activated. It's not necessary to think about what you are reading, as the words are already embedded in your subconscious mind.

Impact Acting uses a combination of specific methods for cold reading and performance-reading. It also takes a holistic approach to developing your individual physical, emotional, and spiritual dynamics. You will be able to do more with your performances if you expand your consciousness. AN ACTOR IS ULTIMATELY MEASURED BY HER OR HIS LIFE-LEVEL AS A PERSON.

You can be sure that the techniques will work if you only practice 20 minutes per week for the first two weeks. Then, it's 20 minutes each week for the second and third weeks. Informal exercises can be integrated into your everyday life throughout the day. This manual is for actors and aspirants looking to improve their craft. The benefits of the disciplined practice of these exercises can be infused into everyday life. Radiating poise is the first step to achieving power, presence, and presence.

LESSON 2

SIMPLICITY

Most acting books and techniques are too complicated for the average reader. It can make it difficult to follow a script in a combat situation. Impact Acting tells what to do and not how it works, as opposed to self-help literature that contains about 10% substance.

While volumes could provide information on the clinical psychodynamics of these techniques in great detail, this is not crucial. It is as easy to follow these instructions as a recipe for baking cake, and it will work. These techniques can be used in a variety of ways, and they are simple to learn. Simple is the key to success, whether you are working in a performance or cold reading mode. You need something involuntary but automatic.

LESSON 3

STAY ACTIVE

"STOP THE MIND - I WANT TO GET OFF!"

Ross Jeffries was a modern philosopher who once said, "The only difference in a homeless guy walking around the street talking all day to himself and anyone else is the fact that he is speaking out loud." People are often unable to control their mind. It seems to move in its own directions, just like a lunatic driver who drives at 90 miles per hour down one-way streets wrong way while you tell it to.

Your mind can only hold one thought or feeling at any given moment. This is the key to focusing. When you can focus on what you have in front of your eyes, your mind will automatically remain still. You'll notice that your inner mental chatterbox stops rambling on endlessly throughout every moment of your waking hours. Instead of feeling numb, you start to feel positive emotions. It becomes clear that your mind doesn't even have the need to be still or focused. Instead, you trust your intuition and spontaneity. This is almost always infallible.

You will find your life much simpler when you source from your higher self. You will make the right decisions regarding characters and events that occur in daily life.

You will only be able to allow in the positive sublime when you have successfully tamed your wild buckingbronco mind. Instead of fear and petty desires, insecurity, and phobias, you choose bliss, love, joy, and light. In this transcendental state you can experience a universal link with all things and everyone. It is possible to project yourself in any situation as another character. You are all that is.

This book is not just a behavioral modification to help you act, as you might be finding out. The book shows you how to create a profound and lasting change in your psychic anatomy. If followed carefully, it can dramatically alter your life. Your core zone is the place where your conscious merges with the subconscious. The process can also produce a magic aura of light.

Chapter 2: Formated Exercises

THE SEVEN-DAY TRAINING WORKOUT

FORMAL PRACTICE includes the 20-minute mental program that is done once per day, for seven days. The picture-recall and breathing exercises are followed up by the visual and/or emotional connection with each word. It is best if you have a set time and location for the workout. Because the mind loves routine and familiarity, it will resist your conscious will to do these mental gymnastics.

The mind is like an animal that can't be controlled. It must be trained to become a stallion, and then it will respond to your commands. It will kick and fight for its own life when it attempts to be disciplined. Your mind and your ego want control over you. You can expect resistance to your mental exercise plan. With an iron will, you must set aside a period of time every day. Remember that you can skip a day and you will still have control of your mind, acting career and life. You must keep showing up.

STEP ONE

DIRECTIONAL EAR MOVEMENT

BREATH RETENTION

This is a psychological concentration exercise that involves eye movement and breathing. It aims to align the emotional and bodily elements into oneself. It is easy to do, takes less than five minutes and is powerful. The eye muscle muscles are given a rest and can be focused. This results in increased energy and more light radiating from your eyes. It also enhances eye movement. This is an important tool for non-verbal communication.

Just by holding your breath, you can quickly relax your mind and stimulate blood circulation to the brain. Retention also improves alpha-wave output which synchronizes left brain activity with right. The result is a more balanced magnet field and a better awareness.

You can get an idea of the power of this therapy by looking at this: There is a rapid increase in psychiatrists who are trained in directional eye treatment called "EMDR" (Eye Movement Desensitization and Reprocessing) as it provides a dramatic improvement in mental wellness, even for victims of trauma.

DIRECTIONS

To begin, extend your jaw as wide as you can and stare at an object cross-eyed. This will give you double vision. For a few moments, close your eyes. Next, visualize a large, red stop sign. Imagine a scene of beauty in nature. A waterfall, a tree blowing through the wind, or an open sky with the moon or sun are some examples. This initial thought will shock the mind. Now you can slow it down and take control.

Point your index fingers up to the corner of your scope. Move it diagonally down towards your vision. You can take a deep breathe and keep it there for as long as you like while you make the eye movements.

Move your finger towards the upper right corner of your vision. Then, bring your eyes and fingers back up to the top. Keep the breath going. Once the fourth cycle has been completed, take deep, slow, and long inhalations. The oxygen-rich air will slowly enter your body. Close your eyes.

Next, do the same four-cycle process, but starting in the upper right corner, then moving to the lower left. Lastly, make a large "X" shape. Once you are done, take a deep breathe and keep it in, closing your eyes.

You can point your finger and eyes directly at the top. Then, make a perfect circle in a clockwise direction while keeping your breathing. Continue the third circle and take a deep breath. You will feel the oxygen coursing through your blood while your eyes are closed. Continue these four circles clockwise.

After repeating this exercise several time, you will eventually be able, with the use of your fingers, to move your eyes to form X,O,and +. Although you may feel lightheaded or faint when you first start this routine (especially if your breathing system is clogged with smoke), this will soon disappear.

Keep working hard, the reward is amazing. It's like having your brain re-energized in just ten minutes. You'll feel balanced both mentally and physically, no matter what situation you find yourself in. You will feel more well in days if you make it a part of your daily routine. It is so powerful. You can only retain your breath while driving if you have passed the lightheaded practice stages. The link between the mental and physical realms is the breath.

You can also use the eye-breath retention exercises to help you sleep naturally. Sleeping pills are only effective for two to 3 days before they cease to be effective. If you don't get the benefit, or if at all, you will suffer from side effects. Scientific studies have shown that 8 hours of rest is the minimum amount of time you need to renew your body and recharge your mind. It's all about energy.

STEP 2

VISUAL RECALL – FORMAL ERCISE

Try to look at a photo, illustration or painting that is interesting or scenic for as long as you can. Keep your eyes open and focus on one part of the picture. Begin to focus on these details by closing your eyes. Keep your eyes open to help you recall them. Once you are confident with the section you have visualized, you can move on and continue the process. Once you've seen the entire picture, don't blink.

Once you have learned the physical aspects and the mental parts of the scene, close your eye. Now mentally project yourself into it as if it were real. You can also practice visualization using your imagination.

If you're in a beautiful natural scene, breathe in the scent of the flowers. Hear the stream moving across the rocks. Hear the crickets and birds singing. Feel the gentle breeze rolling over your cheeks as you feel the warm sun on the face. See the stream sparkle in the sunlight and feel the wind blowing through the tall grass. The picture is made alive by your senses of movement, sensations and wind. You subconscious becomes aware of the reality and you can make it a relaxing 10 minute escape or mini-vacation.

For seven days, you can practice a new picture each morning. Do it. You'll find the ability to be more focused and in control of your life. This will enhance your ability to act and allow you to live life at a higher level. The first day will show a noticeable change in your perspective. You will become more alert to the details and you will make better decisions.

The ability to see through and read people will allow you to see things that were impossible just one week ago. Recalling lines and character-immersion is second nature. It is worth the effort and the rewards. You'll also be able, without any picture, to project your spirit wherever you are. If you have ever experienced astral dreams where you are able see yourself in time and space, this may be a hint that you might have the ability to have this power.

STEP 3

IMAGE / FEELIN

THE SYNCHRONICITY TECHNIQUE

Write a page, paragraph, or section of text. Ideally, it should be narrative or visually descriptive. Then assign each objective word a mental photo and each subjective one a mental feeling. Imagine a sailboat if the word "sailboat" is used. If the word "I", picture yourself. If the word for love is "I", picture yourself in warmth, devotion, affection. If the word means "cold", imagine being in the snow while wearing a bathingsuit. This means that you should not only say the words but also feel them.

Certain words, like prepositions, conjunctions, and some adjectivs, can be hard to see or feel. Therefore, it is important to have an awareness of the sounds of the word (when to, the, if. with, etc.).

You can flash an emotion or image with every word. Now, say the word aloud. Try to exaggerate pitch, inflection, and tonality as if you were reading to two-year-olds. You should use your eyes to communicate the word's meaning.

If you are reading text from the page, make sure to only look down at the copy for enough time to understand a phrase or clause. After that, raise your eyes as if the other person was looking at you. With just one glance, you will be able quickly to comprehend an entire sentence. Additional bonus: Speed dialogue acquisition. Without even reading the script, you can read and perform a cold reading scene of two pages. Even the most experienced professionals don't do this. You will actually enjoy cold readings once you are proficient in this technique. You will be remembered by the casting director for your exceptional memory.

The script that you read will become a moving picture in your brain as if you were actually there. Your subconscious mind (which is 90% of all your power) doesn't differentiate between reality and fantasy. Your brain's mental impulses can be stored in your data bank. So audition readings and performances will be authentic and true because YOU THINK IT'S REAL. Perception is key to acting.

Chapter 3: Informal Exercises In Progress

LESSON 1.

"NOW AWARENESS"

"I", 'you', "he",'she", and? are the most important nouns/pronouns. When you hear or speak these words, you can both feel and see the presence of another person. These are the most important members of the group. We'll be discussing them in the following section. The most used verbs include "am","are", "were", and "was". These verbs suggest a state. "Have", the verbs "has" or "had" signify "in possession of".

You will have a very high level of focus if you only show the images and feelings associated with these most common nouns/pronouns/verbs.

Both informal and formal exercises are important. Each can be done during the day while you go about your daily activities and their impact can add-up quickly. Your perspective can be changed to see new possibilities in your life. Once you are able to master this technique, psychological roadblocks will disappear. This can help serious actors leapfrog the time required to develop their craft. Focus on your goal with your willpower and discipline. Always be present for whatever and whoever is around you. STAY IN NOW ALWAYS

While listening to music, pretend that the song is about your life or an event. Sing the lyrics aloud and let them become part of you for those moments.

When you're eating, pay attention to the colors and textures in your food. You should taste every mouthful. Pay attention to where your body is being touched by the soap, the water or the soapy water. You can watch television and pay attention to details and the action. When the actors speak, try flashing a mental image or feeling for each key word or phrase. You can pretend it's all happening in front of you. Walk for at least 30 minutes. You should be aware of everything around you.

The intricate patterns of leaves and their colors can be seen in the trees.

Feel the warmth of the sun on you , or the chilliness of an Autumn day.

Hear the sounds of the crickets and birds.

Listen to the children's laughter.

When having a conversation, visualize locking in with the other person. This will help you to become more aware of their physical characteristics. Take the time to look at the person and CONNECT on a soul level. Take the time to listen and reflect on every word or phrase. Project a mental movie by giving life to those words. You will immediately notice how much your thoughts will drop when you sync images and feelings with words and thoughts. Many people have thousands of thoughts every day. Some may have some significance, but the majority are made of false imaginations or wistful thoughts, insecurities or subtle fears, and are usually not meaningful.

When you take control of your thoughts and allow only high-quality, relevant thoughts into the mind, they will be less frequent. Though you might say less, every word you say will still have meaning and impact. When your mind slows down, it conserves physical and spiritual energy. You become a permanent loaded gun. Your quiet power can be unleashed when you give your lines in auditions and performances.

If you're serious about being a good actor, you must be willing to do the exercises five days per week. If you skip one day, you will be backtracking. Instead, get back into the exercises and double your efforts for the next day.

Distraction is the biggest problem during this seven day basic training phase. You will find that these exercises aren't something your brain wants to do initially. It will then fight you vigorously. This is why you need to constantly speak out loudly (either alone or with others) the words "image / emotions" and "awareness" along with each keyword. During the seven-day training period you will need to repeat these words daily from morning until night. You may also find it helpful to purchase 3-by-5 flashcards that have the words "IMAGE/FEELING/AWARENESS" in both English and Spanish. One card can be placed in your bedroom, bathroom or kitchen. You can place them in different places each day to make sure they don't get lost or fade into background.

Concentrate on the flash card for several moments before going to sleep. Do this each time you awake during the night. Then, repeat the process in the morning. This will make your subconscious more open and allow you to hit the mark with your words. It is this constant reworking of the subconscious that allows it to convert words into images, feelings, and thoughts throughout the day as the world pulls you in many directions.

The drill involves flashing on an image of key words, or feeling of key phrases (read or spoken by anyone), and being acutely aware on a second to second basis of your surroundings. You may find it difficult initially to focus for extended periods of time. However, keep trying. The flash cards and your own verbal reminders will make it gradually easier. Eventually, the discipline will be like a sport and can even be enjoyable.

Your mind has been controlling for you all your life. You should not expect it will give up on you. Your higher-self must assert itself and claim a superior position to prevail. Although flashing someone's verbal images, feelings, and thoughts every nanosecond can seem time-consuming, it is possible to use your mind to accomplish almost anything. Training can make even slow readers speed up, so don't be discouraged. Our method is much simpler. You will find the image, feeling, awareness, and exercises much more enjoyable within days. Stop getting discouraged, even for a few days. Just start again. You will eventually become a regular practice.

Slow down while talking in order to sync images and feelings with key phrases. Don't be too proud of yourself. Your words will be shorter, but your messages will still have an impact. Don't be slow to speak, just do your best. Most people speak too quickly, so it's okay to slow down and feel the power behind the words. Your ability to understand and align your mind with spoken words will improve the more you practice.

LESSON 2

THINK OF YOUR MIND AS A CAMERA

You can use your mind like a still camera to improve your mental clarity. As you go about your day, notice an interesting object? Close your eyes and try to remember its details. The more you practice, clearer your focus. When you're flashing images to create a scene, it will make you more aware of the reality.

Similar to the other exercises this will become second-nature.

Ironically, it is the same mind which kept you in slavery that becomes your instrument for freedom. Concentration exercises help you to control your mind. The daily exercises will soon become a part of your daily life and will be viewed as a continuous, concentration-acting exercise.

LESSON 3

"I" - "YOU"AWARENESS

Acting involves being connected to yourself and other actors in the scene. One informal exercise that you can include in your daily life is being aware of yourself.

It may seem easy, but this exercise can be extremely powerful. The word "I" should be pronounced as it would be spoken. The brain is where the message originates and it then flows right out of the mouth. It communicates the message well, but it is very ineffective. Now, say "I" and you will experience an awareness of your own being as you do it. This time, "I", although it originates in your brain, is processed in your heart area. This is the feeling part of the body. Your psychic forces propel "I", through theether. You can feel the power in that little word by repeating it dozens of time each day. This is your power.

Next time you speak to someone, use "you" the way you would normally. It flows directly from the brain out to the mouth. It conveys an idea but only in a superficial manner, which is common for most conversations.

Now, look into the eyes of the other person. In that moment you will be able to sense the other person's essence and spirit. This is real communication between soul and soul. What a difference! Your aura will be felt by both the casting director and the other person. It isn't superficial. Others will consider you a person of power and presence.

You must practice the "I' - "you", drill. It requires discipline to be aware of each word you say. Don't forget. If you do, just say the words again, feeling and awareness. If that's not possible, pay attention to the next word in your conversation.

The awareness drill of "I" and "you" continuously teaches your mind to connect with others. You are automatically in your core zone throughout the day. It is especially helpful when you are performing a scene.

Just as you can alter the direction of a large ship's course by turning it one way or another, so can you change your mind. The drill of "I-you" can dramatically improve your acting craft and personal relationships, as it forces you connect and to be real.

LESSON 4

CREATE PRESENCE ENERGY THROUGH BREATHING & FLEXING.

To create charisma, you must combine the "feeling divinity blissful" mindset with the ability to harness the infinite energy of the air that we breathe. The magnetic energy is processed by deep breathing and the stretching of various muscles. STRETCH AND FLEX WITH EVERY STEP! You will feel divinely blissful if you keep deep breaths in and continue to stretch.

If you can do this for one hour, your whole being will be flooded with magnetic energy. In the mirror you'll see some electricity. Imagine how you'd feel and look if it was a habit. YOU WOULD BECOME CHAIRISMA POWERHOUSE.

CONSISTENCY IS THE SECRET TO SUCCESS

You can make these exercises more powerful by re-grooving you subconscious on a daily basis. These exercises are best done consistently and every day. Keep going forward and you'll reach your goal of having a sharp mind. You can be sporadic and it will feel like you're digging a hole a few feet below the ground, only to stop and dig another hole a few yards above. You can spend your whole lifetime digging and working hard but never reach the water. Consistency is key to winning.

Many people who say they want be actors are actually just dabblers. They learn acting techniques, discuss acting, and then they are not able to tear through the layers of illusions and reach the core of their being. This requires determination, hard work, guts, and spirit. You can't afford to let up if you become lazy. Unseen psychological forces are at work. Do not lose heart and just pick up where your efforts left off.

Chapter 4: The Voice

The voice is the amalgamation of a person's spiritual and emotional qualities with a live instrument. A powerful, charismatic voice that touches and inspires the soul is one the greatest gifts of Nature.

UCLA recently revealed that words are the least used communication medium. Amazingly, only 7% is affected by words when communicating between people. The tone of your voice is responsible for 38% of all communication. Think back to your dad calling and threatening you with that tone of voice. You knew you had trouble. You didn't need any other words. 55% is controlled through body language and physiology.

As psychic-level actors, we focus equally on the subconscious minds and audience members. In the formative and informal exercises, you can develop the voice's subtle aspects to their best in a short amount of time.

LESSON 1.

CORK ENUNCIATION

Use a short wine bottle cork to place between your upper & lower teeth. You will then count from 70 to 100. This exercise can also easily be done by curling your index, third and fourth fingers together between your teeth. You can do this alone or with a friend. The practice encourages clear and crisp enunciation. It forces the mouth to widen to allow the lazy tongue to be used. You will see a marked improvement in your diction after a few days of practicing this exercise several times daily. This exercise is vital because it requires that you have excellent diction and pronunciation in order to properly express every syllable or letter, particularly those ending with T's and/or D's. This is the most important characteristic of professional actors.

LESSON 2

TOTALITY EXERCISES

Remember that 38% is made up of communication via tone.

Tonality conveys emotion and intent through words. Your voice will have that warm, human quality. Tonality can be used to express everything. Talking to a small child or dog requires you to use a lot of tonality. It helps them to understand your intent or feeling. In formal exercises, it's a good idea to pretend you're talking to your pet or child. You should pronounce each word with extreme precision and exaggerated tone. This is how to do the enunciation and toneality exercise. It's not exaggerated, as you will discover.

LESSON 3

RESONATION EXERCISES

It is possible to achieve a deep and rich voice by singing opera. You will be forced to generate power using your abdomen, propelled by a resonating dialymm. It moves up from there through the mask of its face, which acts as a speaker.

You can feel the power of vibration when you sing opera. This will increase your resonance. Don Giovanni by Mozart is the best operetta for men. Females can also enjoy any of the Mozart operas. This exercise can also increase the power and projection of your vocal chords, whether you are male or female. You can spend your drive-time singing along to a Mozart operetta CD while you travel. No one will notice that you can sing off-key. If you don't have a CD or audio file of an opera, simply move up and down the scale singing do-ra-me-fa-so-la-te-doo. Keep your hands on each note as you vibrate the diaphragm. Cover two complete octaves.

LESSON 4

EXERCISES IN ABDOMINAL BREATHING

Here's a powerful breathing exercise to increase your lung capacity and resonance.

Take a series of deep, long breaths and slowly increase their frequency. It's like a locomotive starting. You should try to increase the speed of each breath as much as you can. After twenty deep breaths, exhale deeply. You can hold this position for as many as 20 seconds. It may be hard to get into the rhythm. You might feel lightheaded but it is temporary. You can feel the action by placing your hand on the abdomen and diaphragm during this exercise.

Breathing is the most important link between the mind, body, and soul. The technique is simple to implement and gives immediate results. Blood flow to your brain will increase by approximately 25% by decreasing your average breath rate from 15-20 to 10-12. Additionally, anxiety decreases significantly, blood pressure falls, and the brain begins producing alpha-waves that improve balance.

To supply oxygen to your bloodstream, it is very inefficient to take shallow breathes from the tops. This method drains energy from the whole body. To be able to inhale abdominally, you must practice it at all times. You should be able to sit straight and take slow deep, slow breaths.

Chapter 5: Creating Presence

Being present is not an ethereal gift given by God. This is a mathematical process. Anyone who is willing to follow the formula precisely can generate it. Your presence comes from a force field that radiates energy and psychical energy from your inner center. It is this same center that creates your aura as well as the sparkle in you eyes.

Presence is about being focused from your core area. It's defined by your power. charisma. light. energy. All of these factors translate into the magic in a performance. As you continue to perform the formal as well as informal exercises, your presence is being created. The following technique will give you an immediate boost of psychic energy. This will allow you to transcend your ego and create a powerful presence that will propel your performance.

LESSON 1.

INSTANT CHARISMA

PROCESS WITH QUICKCHARGE

You can think of a moment in your life where you felt total bliss. Or maybe you just received some unexpected good luck in a financial or personal area. One example could be the time you felt completely loved by your parents and a mate, an amazing sexual moment or anything that always makes you smile. You may feel an exhilaration and excitement filling your mind. Now hold that feeling for a few second, just like it is for the very first time. Take that feeling and make it more intense. Enjoy it for several second. It will flow through your bloodstream, spreading throughout your entire body, until it becomes bliss. Enjoy the divine bliss you feel and keep it as a frame of reference to help you recall it at all times.

If you're unable to invoke this feeling of blissful joy right away, it could be a sign your heart and consciousness may be partially closed. It doesn't matter if you have to keep trying, it won't take long before you get the feeling again. This will bring you joy and only then will it be truly alive.

LESSON 2

EXTENDED SYSTEM

BLISS. LIGHT. LOVE.

Although the quick energy of presence is helpful for auditions, performances, and other purposes, the goal is to be present all the time and continue to produce and conserve psychic energies. This means a fundamental shift of how you perceive and respond to every person and thing in your day. You will be required to exceed the normal patterns of human behavior and demonstrate dedication to acting. A serious actor must make the creating presence process and the practice of the formal as well as informal exercises part of everyday life.

When you generate charisma (or a sense of presence), it erupts from your eyes like twinkling stars and affects anyone within its reach, including the camera. It becomes part of your essence the more you keep this bliss feeling. For the past few minutes, you may have felt better than in a long while. Why not continue feeling that way for the rest of your life? To stop having random, unfounded thoughts all day, you just have to be focused and stop focusing. It is not because of something that happened, but because of the rush.

Mentally visualise LIGHT as the sun. Visualize yourself radiating warmth and light on everyone. Focusing on the light will make you shine a beautiful, enticing glow on everyone who meets you.

FEELS LOVE for everything. You shouldn't judge people or things that you see. Watch your life change when you love them. Instead of thinking constantly, try to feel bliss, see light, and feel love. Alternate the three, and your life will soon become one continuous rush. The result is a person of peaceful power.

Chapter 6: Stress – The Charisma Killer

Energy and stress can be counterproductive. Energy and drive are drained faster by stress than anger, fear, anxiety, guilt, and their caustic cousins. All negative emotions are draining your life force. If you ever feel an overwhelming feeling of fear or anger, take a look in the mirror. You will be amazed at how much your face has changed because of all the toxic substances that circulate through your bloodstream. Even mild anxiety and low-stress forms of stress can drain vitality in the same way a car battery is short-circuited. Some forms, like competitive sports, may be beneficial. It can be difficult and exhausting to remove unhealthy stress. However, that is what makes life worth living. What is left is the REAL you after stress and anger have gone?

Your body must be in sync with you and your energy must be high to perform well in order for you to act effectively. Stress and its allies - anger and desire - can erode your energy reserves. They also cause a reduction in the nervous system which can lead to a loss of body harmony and control, which then impacts motor and spatial capabilities.

The more you practice the charisma, formal, and informal exercises, the more powerful your protective magnetic field. When you are consistent with the exercises, until they become a way of life, your magnetic force field will be strong enough to repel all negativity. You will not be bothered. It's like having an immunization shot for emotional pain. With this, you can navigate through life's obstacles like an Arctic Ocean icebreaker. It's all about the mind. So if you use the mind against the mind, you can win the very battle for your life. This is possible if you just follow the directions.

Chapter 7: The Cold Reading Audition

To schedule yourself to audition for a part at the end of the audition is the first step. First impressions are always the strongest so make sure you audition for the part as soon as possible. Listening to music on the radio can help you get ready. You can project yourself fully into the song by flashing images or feelings to the lyrics as if it were your first person.

LESSON 1.

INSTANT RELAXATION SERVICES

When auditioning, most actors feel anxious or nervous. You can relax and stay focused by practicing these simple techniques to counter anxiety.

Sit upright, take deep, slow abdominal breaths, and exhale slowly.

1. Slowly and deeply breathe and pay attention to the process while you read your scene. The best way to do this is to hold your

breath for at least a few seconds, then let it out.

2. While you are walking from your car into the casting room, grab a small object and stare at it cross-eyed about ten times. Now close your eyes. Visualize a large stop sign and shout "STOP!" internally or externally.

3. Now think of several zeros, with nothingness in between them. This will only take a few moments and will greatly slow down your mind's momentum.

4. You can get new blood to your brain and your juices flowing by touching your toes.

This drill will help place you in a zone that is focused and has energy for the reading.

LESSON 2

INSTANT CHARISMA – QUICK CHARGE

(As per the previous section).

You can think of a moment in your life where you were completely happy. Perhaps you received some unexpected good luck in a financial or personal area. Another example could be when your parents, or a partner loved you. Think of a joke, or anything that makes you smile. A sexual experience that is exhilarating may be a possibility. It may be a feeling of exhilaration in your head. Now hold that sensation for a few second, as if it were happening for the very first. You can now take that feeling and make it more intense by taking the time to savor it for several minutes. Feel it rushing through your bloodstream, spreading to your entire being until you reach the bliss.

You should keep this divine feeling up until you come face-toface with your casting host. Then, take a moment to look each person in their eyes, and then blast them with your bliss energy (charisma).

LESSON 3

THE REHEARSAL OF AND READ--WITH THE IMAGEFEELINGTECHNIQUE

One to three pages of scene description are provided for you to review. It is important to take a moment to look at the scene and then flash your feelings and images. This repetitive process will make it difficult to focus, sometimes in less than a minute. It will also embed the entire scene in your subconscious, including all of the emotional subtleties that are associated with each word. The process of flashing images, feelings and thoughts with each word is much faster if you have completed both formal and informal exercises.

"I," "he," and "he" are the most important lines of dialogue in a scene. You should be able see yourself mentally and feel your presence when you say "I". Use the word "you" to address someone, regardless of whether they are a casting director or a photographer. If you do not know who the person is, then create an image.

Each time you read the script, focus less on it as you try to memorize the words. This will be easier than you realize if your attention is focused. Flash images, feeling arbitrarily attached to key words or phrases of your part are also helpful. Expand on the other person's part. This is equally important.

This will create a real-life motion picture in your brain, almost as if you were actually there. If you can quickly go through the scene, and only occasionally glance down to catch up on the dialogue, then you are ready. The scene should be your only reality.

If the casting director offers additional interpretations of a scene, you should be sure to use key words or phrases to display images and feelings. These thoughts could be spontaneously generated by your own imagination.

As such, you should think of any director's notes that are attached to a scene in the first-person as if they were coming from your personal perceptions. Also, subtext refers to the character's inner thoughts as well as motivations that are not in line with the dialogue. These thoughts should be seen in the first-person instead of the third.

It is important that the character being described is always you in the first person. Not someone separate from you in third person. This requires that you make fundamental changes in your reality-base from the moment you enter the casting room. You are the only person on the screen. There is not a casting director. There are no actors. There are only the circumstances and people in the scene. The scene is your life, your reality.

Lock your eyes to the person reading the previous lines before you begin the reading. If a camera is being used, you should read to the closest eye to the camera. This is vital and it will make all the difference when they play it again.

The script should be held below your neckline to ensure you don't block any part of your face. Keep your head up and your eyes open to grab your lines.

You will feel and see the feelings and images as you repeat the words. You have pre-programmed the mental computer in the outside preparation room. Now, just say the words and listen for the emotional impulses. This is your cold-reading technique. You simply need to say and listen to the dialogue. What could be easier? No matter what your preference, you will find it real and believable.

As you leave the room after the reading is over, remember to look back at the door and thank the casting directors. No matter how good you are at that part, the casting director will still remember you and be able to cast you again.

LESSON 4

CREATING THE MALIC

It's amazing to witness an actor reach deep within their soul to create an experience that truly moves you. These spontaneous impulses arise automatically when actors are in an unthinking, feeling-intense zone that allows for them to be themselves.

Your infinite source will take control of your ego. First, trust it completely. Focus on the role and not on how you sound. You can then do the exact same thing with your lines. Feel completely relaxed but emotional tightening. If you are naturally in an altered state, you can accomplish anything.

Acting's most basic commandment is to "Thou shalt never bore", and the unpredictability of acting is always thrilling. Furthermore, being real will ensure that you never bore even when performing a scene that seems unnatural. Even though you may only say a few words, your silent power is the most powerful. Quiet water runs deep.

Magical performance moments are possible when you live life from a higher awareness. Since you are already part of your normal consciousness, it is easy for you to easily slip into your power center zone.

The operative watchword to acting is ENERGY. This refers to how to create and conserve energy. No matter how boring or stupid they may seem, you will want it. INTENSITY Is the Key. It's all about the big reward - the moments when you transcend yourself. There is no other way. So don't be a cheater on yourself. It is this high vibratory, psychic, and/or physical energy that will inspire your infinite creativity. LET YOUR OWN ENERGY FIRE THE MAGIC ALONE.

Chapter 8: Presence - Charisma Thru Mind Overload

The general rule of thumb is that any thought, feeling, or act that expands your consciousness generates presence. Negative thoughts, remarks, and actions are what contract consciousness. The mind-body-spirit entity functions in a similar way to a battery, which is being charged and depleted in different degrees every second. You radiate light and energy more if you have a positive, spiritual and physical charge.

These spiritual laws can greatly accelerate that charge. While the negative counterparts to each law have the opposite effect, they are key spiritual laws. We aren't going on a joyride to the new age. Our goal is not to disintegrate the old mental layers. We are trying to give you the energy and clarity to act. It's a self help crash course.

LESSON 1.

THE ART of POSITIVE THINKING

Since positivity is all-encompassing it is the best and most fundamental law. It is easy to talk and share positive thinking. But it is quite difficult to put it into daily practice. Because the unexpected is always coming, it is not hard to be optimistic. The entire chapter on Positive Thinking will show you how to keep a positive attitude even in difficult situations.

"The mind is its very own place." It can make both a heaven and a hell of its own heaven.

- John Milton

Everybody has a deep reservoir of joy and bliss at the soul level. This is unobstructed by many filters that are created by ego processing. Every day we are bombarded daily with small annoyances and anxieties as well as unexpected events which can cause fear and stress. The majority of these negatives, while insignificant, are like tiny weights on an ophthalmologist's scale. These negatives can quickly add up and start to affect your outlook. Ninety-nine% of the times, things don't seem nearly as bad, but our ego tends amplify them. It seems that this mass of negative energies doubles in force every hour until it becomes all-consuming.

As an actor and as a happy individual, you need to get rid of any negative thoughts that are lodged in your head and stop new complexes from developing. It is possible to overcome negative encounters that you have with people, events, and/or perceived events with a simple and workable coping strategy. This method is useful in the first stages of an encounter to combat negative impressions, before they become more severe and take over a life of its own.

The reason this technique is so effective is that it bypasses the usual reactive trauma process and taps directly to your reserve to expand the brain. The negative can be negated and all that remains is the positive. Not to be ignored, but to confront the source of the problem head-on and dissipate it.

LESSON 2

THE SECRET TECHNIQUE

HOW TO BE POINTIVE DURING A DVERSITY

When you meet any type of adversity or perceived adverse event for the first, make sure you immediately think it is the worst thing you have ever experienced. Consider it the end, worse than death, even if you are only experiencing a minor inconvenience. You may feel intense anger, despair, or fear for only a few minutes. The ego sees that the situation doesn't seem very serious and can no long sustain such extreme negativity. This forced process helps to subliminate the normal reactive patterns by quickly bringing it up to a point and popping their bubble.

As soon as you notice the negative momentum in the mind begin to decrease and the initial hit, whether it is real or imagined, your mind will suddenly shift in the opposite direction. You'll be able to pretend that you just won the lottery. Your mind will believe this fear or perceived negative caused you to win, which is the greatest thing to ever happen to you.

Double that feeling until you feel joy. Use that concentrated positive energie to blast out the dark negative mass.

The mind can only hold one thought at a given moment, so keep that feeling locked in, regardless of how negative it might try to get in. This is when your gut and willpower are needed. This could be a pivotal moment in your entire life. If anger, fear or a negative feeling temporarily overtakes you, then just go back through the despair to joy process until it goes away.

You now face your long-time nemesis the negative ego. This is your chance for victory, so don't let this chance slip away. You can do it with all of your positive energy. This moment could be the turning point of your life.

The Adversity, or perceived negative event, can turn out to be the greatest thing that has ever happened to you. This is because it has given you the opportunity to see who you really, truly are. It has allowed you to overcome fear and anger. This is a huge victory by itself and far exceeds the negative effect of actual adversity. You will be able to resolve the matter more clearly and effectively without mental agitation. Continue to practice the technique with increasing difficulties until you reach a point where you can automatically feel joyful when faced with adversity.

ASK YOUR MIND FOR HELP.

What could be better than that? The more things are difficult, the more you feel. It's like getting an injection for the pains around the world. No matter how rich or poor you are, what success means to you, your love or hate, who you are or what you don't like, you will always feel happy and peaceful. YOU WILL BE HAPPY ONLY FOR THE PURPOSE OF HAPPINESS--THIS IS BEING. All those positive feelings that keep flooding into your subconscious will eventually dissolve and neutralize any negative impressions. Your ego is patiently waiting for a catalyst, before it rises up with a vengeance and sabotage your efforts. You must not allow it to have the chance.

It is possible to reprogram the emotional hot buttons so that even a catastrophe does not send you in a tailspin. You can start reconditioning yourself by using small, negative events as well as annoyances to recondition your thought process. You will start to notice tangible changes almost immediately. Each of these small victories will quickly add up and provide the foundation to deal with larger negatives. Because the accepted norm is so small, you will see a significant improvement in your overall quality and life.

This should not be confused with the common drill in which you are asked to react in a neutral fashion to a positive or not at all. This tactic simply allows the issue to go, allowing it to become more powerful such as anger, fear, and/or a physical illness. To subliminate the problem, we must first be fully aware.

We respond with intense positivity, because the problem we are trying to conquer is our negative mind. Additionally, any negative impulse can cause more harm to your mind or body than the actual event. No matter how horrible things may seem, trust that it is in your best interest. When you look back at your entire life, you will find that nearly everything you have experienced was for the good. The lessons you learned from the adversity have enabled you to move forward to where you currently are.

Even if your stress tolerance is not high, this technique will allow you to experience a state of lasting happiness. Bliss is an emotion that can be experienced in any situation.

It is possible to live heaven on earth. You can be happy if you don't want to be. This is because any event that triggers a positive emotion, no matter how negative, will make you feel happier.

You can eliminate all the negatives and still have the positive.

LESSON 4

Live from your FEELING MODE

Living from the feeling mode instead of the constant thought mode will allow you to feel divine magnetism and glide through life with a sense of bliss. You don't need to think much. Your instincts are your guide and you always seem to do the right decision.

Because the world is projected by the mind, it's important to feel instead of think, thinking and feeling. Your world can become a wonderful dream. If you can radiate positive, forceful thought wave, you can influence the minds of others, even from afar. Your mind vibrates and activates positive karma from past experiences, resulting in good luck. This strong positive energy will help you build mental power and flexibility that will enable you to excel at work.

An actor should try to exude a sense of happiness that makes it almost impossible to see the negative sides of the material world. You can tackle trials head-on, without becoming caught up in them or creating new complexes.

Chapter 9: Universal Laws

These spiritual laws can help to clear your mind, and prevent you from creating new complexes. Only then, you can be open to acting and living. Many of these principles are essential in self-help books as they can profoundly impact us.

LESSON 1.

THE LAW OF ATTRACTION

This book is directly and directly predicated on law of attraction. It states that whatever you have in your mind will become reality. You can make a scene your reality by locking in a picture, feeling for words or feeling for a scene. Our mind is like an electric magnet that transmits mental waves of intent to all elements of the universe every day. People and circumstances attract according to the thought vibrations.

People who think positive thoughts about love, light, happiness, abundance, and growth experience a similar reality. Conversely, those who project anger, fear, anxiety, and despair create a living hell. Most people have a mix of positive and negative thoughts. Mediocrity is their daily reality. A positive mind attracts more positive thought. This in turn attracts positive people and events that are good for you. This is why more good fortune seems to be associated with good luck.

Your intention is enhanced by clarity of vision, emotional willpower and clarity of purpose. You will likely achieve your goal if you believe in it and are committed to it. Expect little if you are unable to see the big picture and lack willpower. Doubt and other negative emotions reduce willpower. You are not the only thing that can affect your resolve. These include smoking, lying, excessive television viewing, movie watching, idle talk, smoking and poor diet.

Positive alternatives to these negative behaviors include honesty, few words, and good health habits. This includes extensive cardiovascular and resistance training, weight training, and good communication. All these factors help you to develop strong willpower which is key to making your dreams come true.

Focusing on what you don't desire can lead to you focusing on the things you do want. However, you might be able get it by giving attention and energy. For a balanced life, don't forget the old adage "hear not evil, see nothing evil, speak none evil". You must eliminate all things that are not helpful or beneficial to your higher wellbeing. You can find something positive in everyone.

Your future will be shaped by your inner-dialogue, hour-to-hour thoughts, and minute-to-minute actions. It is important to pay attention to your inner-dialogue and take time to reflect on the day. If you are able to practice these ongoing, informal exercises, you will feel blissful all the time. It will make your life a paradise on Earth, regardless of your external circumstances.

Most people are unable to understand why others see them differently than they do. This includes casting directors and audiences. This can be due to low or moderate self-esteem, which is again a result their minute-to-minute thoughts throughout their lives.

You are in direct communication at a psychical level with others, whether you like or not. Because of this, you are perceived as authentic and real. It is impossible to project an image that you are not, if you believe you are someone else.

It is important to believe that others will see you differently than you do. You will feel fake if you try to convince your self with positive affirmations. Although you tell yourself, "I'm strong "...", your critical mind is telling you that "No, you aren't...No, you're not ..."

The best way to communicate with your subconscious without relying on the mind-saboteur is by writing down one or two affirmations longhand before you go to bed. You can then take a few minutes to study them and whisper them into your heart. The subconscious enjoys being whispered at, much like a baby appreciates the gentle whisper of its mother. You can whisper to yourself whenever you need a true friend to have a conversation.

The critical mind cannot intercept your new impressions while you are asleep. Instead, they can pass through the gate to start resonating in the night. The subconscious can access itself to re-script its data bank by combining visual communication from your handwriting.

Affirmations need to be clear and concise in order for subconscious to understand. It is best to limit your words to one or two words. The subconscious mind doesn't recognize negative words like "not", so use only positive words. If it does not, the subconscious mind will mistake "I don't weak" for "Im weak" and reaffirm what you want.

One way to improve your self-image and attitude is to pretend you're someone with immense power and presence. It could be someone famous, living or deceased. It could also be someone you are familiar with who exhibits desirable character traits. A complete character study should be done. It should include details about how the person talks, behaves with others, their posture and other characteristics. Take photos of your loved one and display them in key areas around the house. Keep photos of people you care about in your most used drawers. You can always keep a printed copy in your pocket.

As you become one, imagine your subject's facial expressions merging with yours. Your subconscious mind will be most open to your ideas when you are awake and before you go back to sleep.

As you go about your daily activities, pretend that everything is part of a movie.

As an actor playing a part, you can rationalize how you behave and your ego will stop trying to control it. Ego prefers the status-quo and is afraid of any changes that would diminish its importance or make it extinct. Ego is not meant to be controlled but to control you. It is therefore necessary to fool the ego as all that we teach is intended to endanger its existence.

Keep acting the same way even though you may think you're just pretending, and you will eventually get what you want. Since the subconscious is unable to distinguish between real and pretend, these new impressions and powers will gradually start to manifest themselves in your involuntary behaviors and actions. You can become it if it is your will to act as it. It is our law that attracts.

LESSON 2

THE LAW of LOVE AND FORGIVENESS

Send light love and not judgment to everyone you meet. You can experience intense love, even though there are no objects or people around you. Do it because it feels so good. Feel this love by imagining white light flooding your body from above. It will make every cell in you tingle.

Forgive! Forgive! Forgive! Let go of any anger you may have for anyone past or present. These feelings are deeply ingrained in your subconscious where most power is, so it will be challenging. It will take a strong argument from your ego to forgive someone who has hurt or harmed you. But, this will have a profound effect on clearing your mind. The benefits that you'll reap over time will far surpass the transgressions committed by the person.

Anger is hidden deep within the brain. Therefore, we need to use language that our subconscious can understand. A simple command to the conscious mind to forgive someone is often ineffective. This method is extremely effective and easy to use.

You can forgive anyone you want. Start by thinking about yourself. Next, think about the people you would like to forgive. Each offender will make it easier because you'll feel a subtle relief once you have cleared out the poison. Start with faith and sheer willpower. Soon, you will be able to see how the law works.

The forgiveness technique

* Write the name of the person, and briefly describe what he/she did to you.

* Please describe how that act affected your life and feelings.

* Write down that the person is forgiven completely.

* Visualize the person and whisper thoughts of unconditional forgiveness. You can then let them go into light and love while they smile to let the world know that you are okay.

* Set the piece on fire in a safe location and let it burn.

* Do the same thing except that you substitute the names of the people and/or animals you have injured and ask for forgiveness.

THE LAW OF GIVING

It is possible to instantly increase the light and psychic energy in your mind by giving back to the community. You will experience a clearer vision and greater willpower when you help others, no matter how much it is appreciated.

LESSON 3

LAW OF LAUGHTER

A good belly laugh will open your eyes and make you feel better. It's easy to show your charisma by smiling or laughing. As we mentioned, if you can keep your energy on the right side of laughing, you'll shine light and energy that will last you the duration of the scene.

Laugh at yourself, and everyone else. Start having more fun when you laugh. Each particle in the universe around you is vibrating joyfully. Do not lose the joy that is within you. Get rid of the burdens you have been carrying all these years. Just get off it! Celebrate every precious moment. When you can make a joke and have fun, it is a sign that you are beginning to clear.

LESSON 4

THE LAW OF HUMILITY, AND THANKFULNESS

These spiritual laws are able to expand and clearen consciousness more than most people realise. You will find that your charisma and presence increases, which will lead to an ego-driven tendency to gain weight, which will ultimately hinder any gains. It is important to constantly acknowledge the source of any new powers you have in order to remain humble. All the time, give thanks to God, Nature, or Spirit for everything. Keep thanking for all the little things you encounter throughout the day. You can be thankful for your eyesight, hearing, and the ability to walk and speak during non-event times. Being thankful will help you keep your gains and allow for grace to grow.

There are many other names for this euphoric, reverberating sensation. It is sometimes called the Holy Spirit by many Christian sects. Samadhi is a name for it in eastern religions. Nearly all religions have their own terms.

Sometimes, we can feel the same bliss when we listen to a song or music that vibrates in our souls. It is the essence of life and the foundation for spiritual, emotional and physical healing. Euphoric bliss, a spontaneous and powerful force for creating charisma and personal presence, is the reason. It works quickly and consistently, elevating you to a level that will make you feel even more joy.

LESSON 5

ALWAYS TELL YOUR TRUTH, AND KEEP UP YOUR WORD

Telling the truth is the best way to keep your conscious clear and your subconscious intact. This rule is only possible in extremely rare situations, such as when you are forced not to hurt someone's feelings. It is crucial to remember your word even if it seems insignificant.

Tell someone you are going do something. Explain why.

If you don't do it, your subconscious mind notices that you aren't doing what you said you would do. You can make your subconscious stop taking your words seriously if you repeat it enough times, even small ones. If your conscious mind wants something, your subconscious will usually go in another direction to defeat your goals. Don't be dishonest and keep your word to people. This is how you will treat yourself.

Chapter 10: Introduction To Acting

I welcome you to the exciting journey of learning and acting. The art of acting can be an exciting and rewarding journey. It will always be unpredictable. To me, this requires three fundamental values: discipline, dedication and enthusiasm. You already have the key to making this transition easier if you have all three. First you have to learn how to use a toolset in order for you to move forward with your acting. These tools will serve as your guide and are easy to use. Once you have mastered them, everything will happen automatically.

My first year in drama school was when one of my acting instructors told me to get up and cross the room one by one. Everyone wondered: "What's that?" We are going to be walking like models. When we stopped doing our walks, it was obvious that the truth was out. He pointed out three crucial things to us. The first was the fact that half of us had laziness in our bodies. Bad posture and bad walking meant that half of us were not able to move properly. Second, because we were aware we were being exposed, our bodies were tight. We wanted to be strong. Instead, we were doing precisely the opposite. He also noticed that neither of us was natural.

Then, we added a very simple thing. Our tutor asked us just after we finished walking to introduce themselves by saying, "Hi, my names Gabriel" for example. We wanted to make an impression so most of the students said their names and showed that they were confident. These were three very important lessons that we learned very quickly. Relax, be truthful and simple.

Perhaps you have heard the expression, "The voice is the actor's most valuable instrument." There's a reason. Magnetically assembling many pieces into one performance gives the voice credibility. One could even say that the eyes are the most valuable place in a film. Later, I will share a few exercises to help you warm up your voice, control and project it.

Chapter 11: Breathe Through Diaphragm

We breathe through our diaphragm when we're babies. This allows for a higher quality of life in many ways. As we age, we inhale more through our chests, which means that we are able to inhale from the chest. It is best to relax, place your hands on your stomach and inhale.

Here are some exercises to help you control your breath. Begin by strengthening your diaphragm until it can handle long sentences. Consider yourself an actor if you are able to deliver long speeches with one breath or in such a controlled manner that everyone can understand what you do, then you have a formidable weapon in your arsenal.

Exercise 1

Slowly and controlled, exhale. You can repeat this process several times until your breathing becomes effortless. Continue until you have complete control. I recommend slowing your exhalation, making an "S" sound. You can control the flow of air much better if you make it soft. You can exhale as forcefully when you reach the point where there are very few oxygen drops. Now stand straight up and take five deep breathes. They all come from your diaphragm. Slowly loosen up, then slowly bend over your knees. Next, fold your hands in a half-circle, keeping your hands free.

Relax, take five deep breaths, and then slowly, gently, return to your original position.

Exercise 2

Then we move onto the next exercise. We continue to keep the same perspective. We make sure that our legs are the same height as our shoulders. We begin shifting our weights from one foot to another. Choose the foot that you want to inhale. The other will be used for exhalation. You can do this for about a minute. Take a deep breathe, bring your foot to the centre of the stance, and exhale. When you have exhausted all the air, make a forced S sound.

Exercise 3

The following exercises will help you release your mask. A mask is the lower portion of our face. Before we can perform, it is necessary that the room be unblocked and readily available. The first exercise involves the lips. We start to tremble. We repeat this a few more times. Then, we use our mouth to produce sounds. Then you can start with ma and me, mi, mo and mou / Ta, Te,ti.to, tou / Ka, Ke, Ki, Ko, Kou. You can't do these exercises if your diaphragm isn't working. These exercises are vital. You must also incorporate them into your everyday life. It's not possible to start it just because you're about to perform. It is not going to work. Because you will use it in your theatre performances, you must also learn the function of projecting our voice. You need to be able to do this without sounding too loud. First, you need to determine the range and depth in your voice. Your diaphragm should support them both. Start with small beats on your chest. Next, start humming. Slowly, open our mouths and make the following sounds:

Mmmmmmmmmmmaaaaaaaaaaaaah

Mmmmmmmmmmmeeeeeeeeeeeeeh

Mmmmmmmmmmmiiiiiiiiiiiiiiiiiiiiiiiiiiiiiiiiiiiiiih

Mmmmmmmmmmooooooooooooooooh

Mmmmmmmmmouuouououououuuuuuuuh

Once we open our mouths, one of our hands is used to visually guide our voice.

Exercise 4

The final exercise is tongue movements. To practice tongue movement, you must circle clockwise. Take your tongue out, then in again, and finally you fold it and flip it open like a lizard.

That was it. You are now ready to go. Flexibility is another thing we need. An awakened body needs mobility and energy. These exercises will help you be a better performer on the stage or in film. You feel intense anxiety before each performance. That's perfectly normal. It is called functional angst. When you hear the words action or see the stage, your stress magically vanishes, and becomes unlimited energy. You're sharp. You can do things you wouldn't normally be able to do while sitting down with friends for a cup of tea. Your mind is faster than normal and you are more aware. When you perform, your mind is connected to another world. We will discuss this later.

More exercises can be used to activate the body

Exercise 1

We begin to smack each other all over. We begin by smacking our bodies all over, starting with our thighs front and rear. Next we move to our calves.

Let us bring our belly to our chest, lower back, chest, chest, upper back and shoulders. Then, let's get on with the arms.

Exercise 2

Another exercise is to jump from one spot to the next, pretending you have a jumping rope in both of your hands. After you have found a rhythm, or pace that is comfortable for you, continue the exercise for two minutes. Now, shake your legs and move your hands. Your head should be moving clockwise and backwards.

Exercise 3

Do small jumps while punching in front. Keep making small, slow punches

Exercise 4

Get down on your toes and climb for a moment.

Exercise 5

Another minute in a rocking chair

Exercise 6

Bring your feet together and gradually unfold your legs to your final position. You can reach the centre by extending your hands towards it.

Exercise 7

Now, lean to your left and then to you right. Reverse your position. That was it. You are now done.

Relaxation

Relaxation is the first thing an actor needs to do. This is something you may not realize. Relaxing doesn't necessarily mean you will fall asleep. We are referring to your body being more relaxed and able to take control of itself. Relaxing your body allows you to better understand and feel the tension. Any tension in your body is usually obvious because one of the parts is twitching, or something isn't right at this moment.

The body can't express emotions and feelings when it is under tension. The body must follow the action or it will be a poor performance. Let's get to the best exercises for relaxation. I call it the ball tour. This exercise can help you relax, and at the same, it allows you to have complete control over every part of yourself. You lie down and now, listen only to my voice.

Ball Tour Exercise

You will need to take five deep inhalations from your diaphragm. Next, close your eyes. Take another five deep inhalations. Now, imagine that you have a small ball the size and shape of a grape. Keep your eyes on your diaphragm and focus your breath on it. You can imagine the ball being held in your right palm. Imagine the texture of this ball. Its weight is similar to a clod. Now, the ball falls slowly from your hands and heads to your palm. Now, slowly, the ball moves towards your wrist. Then, the wrist feels like it's massaging your wrist. This is where you feel some pressure.

This massage can relax your wrists, making your hand more flexible and reducing tension. It continues on its journey to your wrist and continues until it reaches your elbow. It reaches your tricep and continues to your elbow. You feel the ball's pressure much more than its actual mass. It moves towards you and remains there for 10 second. You feel the ball getting colder and begin to feel it on your skin. The ball now begins to create circles on the affected area, and it is becoming warmer. The ball now has the exact same temperature as your skin. Next, it will move upwards to your neck along its circumference. Directly impacts your chin.

From there, it moves vertically to your forehead. It stays where it is. As long as the ball is on your forehead you can find the balance that will keep it there. Stable. It feels like it is trying to slip away. But you stay focused on the ball. The ball stays still. Now the ball glows white and radiates light. This light acts as energy to feed your body and relax all tension. It gives you just enough energy to help you accomplish your goals as an actor. Nothing is unnecessary.

After you are done, the ball will return to its original form and move to the other side. Next, the ball will move to your triceps. Then it will turn to your lower back and eventually to your bicep. Once the ball has moved to your wrist and is at the tip of you fingers, you will grab it again using your thumb and index. Place it on the top of you chest, where it joins with your neck. Next, begin to slowly roll your stern line towards your diaphragm toward your abdominals. When you reach the end, the ball starts rolling back at your lower back. It then slowly moves on your spine.

Each movement of the ball is felt as it crosses each vertebra. Once the ball touches you neck, it will glide back down to your hips. The ball now lies on your right foot. The ball will then roll down around your leg to reach your ankle, and finally your foot. The ball then goes back up and moves to your left leg. Then it moves to your left leg. Next, take 5 more deep, diaphragmatic inhalations and you will open your eyes.

The importance the solar plexus plays in acting

The functionality and power of the solarplexus lies in the perception that all the intentions are coming through it. The primary energy driving all of the actions performed by actors is the sun plexus. By giving an area to this, he was giving actors something to be focused on and committed to. Our movement is grace because it should be guided there. This gives us total control of what we do.

While it can be uncomfortable and strange at first, it allows actors to feel secure and confident in every move they make. The high abdomen houses the solarplexus, the seat for power. The voice is a vital instrument for actors. But to make the most of it, the body must be aligned in such a manner that all chakras can work together. It is important to understand how to control your body during movement classes.

A common phrase that is repeated often and clearly describes it is that your body posture must be like an imaginary string pulling you from your head. Even if your body is straightening now, the best way to achieve the grace of confident walking or an act is to feel all the energy in the solar plexus. Then, have something drag you from there. You will not be consciously aware of it at first. But, once you get used to it, it will become clearer that it makes sense for you to drive it.

Expressions

This is where theatre and film differ. We want our expressions and moves to be more visible in theatre. We are often exposed to the audience. We don't own a camera that can take us up close. To make a statement, you need to use every movement and expression. You must convey the message to the audience as a character.

Mirrors are a great way to familiarize yourself with your facial expressions. Mirrors are a great way to get familiar with your expressions. These are just four examples. You can try out different approaches and different ways. Playing is a way to express your happiness. It can be expressed in many ways. It could be a smile or a exhale. Limit yourself to nothing.

Perception

Perception is an essential part of being an actor. Without perception, it is impossible to be an actor. You will quickly realize that being a complete actor means having everything. But you can never have it all. Because we must continue to practice, improve our craft, and thirst for knowledge just as we did the first day, it is important that we never have everything.

Every star actor you admire and know has said it at the very least several times throughout their careers. Training an actor is never finished. Perception is how well we can understand specific things during a performance. How well our perceptions of the performance, environment and set-up are. The definition of perception is to see everything around and within you. It's like a sponge that absorbs everything so you know exactly what to do and where to stand.

Memorization

Memorization can be described as the ability or skill to memorize a text. Every actor is different in how they learn the lines. Some actors are more proficient at memorizing than others. It is important to be able to read and understand the lines well enough to be able to tell the stories in different ways. Let me be more specific. It will not become organic if it is just something you know by heart. It will remain a simple line.

History is something we can recall by heart. Different people have different methods of learning lines. Most actors will use this method to learn lines. They can be repeated loud with their partner. It can be hard to perform a scene by yourself if you are not accompanied. There is no problem with monologues. This is the most important part of the job, as we go through the script and play over and again at the table.

Even if you do not read the entire book, that doesn't mean you are done learning. Clear your head of stress, tension and pressure. These are counter-productive and make the process more difficult. You can use the relaxation methods we've already mentioned to help you.

To stretch, find a peaceful and quiet space that is free from distractions. I like to go to a park to do my lines once, without any particular patterns. Then, I start stretching out by saying the lines aloud.

Break down the learning. For example, set goals. Two teams of lines can be learned in 30 minutes, or 20 minutes. Your lines can be recorded to a Dictaphone, or phone. Listen to them when you get home from work or at home. It is best to listen just before you fall asleep, or wake up. This is because your brain is in Alpha waves and is more likely to absorb the information. Next, sing the lines. You can use them in opera, musical theatre, pop, or rap. Use different accents and voices.

Anything that makes your mind more active and easier to absorb. This is a fun and stress-free way to learn them and remember them.

People find it helpful to write down their thoughts. Try it, and let us know how it goes. Another option is to stand before a wall and talk your points. You will be more focused if your lines are near the wall. If you listen to them, they will become even easier to remember.

Confidence

It is the first step to acting. Actors get exposed all the time. He has the element that "I'm here so you can find me". An actor can be seen not only in his physical appearance, but also in his emotional state. When you decide to become an actor, it is essential that you accept the role. Accept that your path will expose you and allow you to be judged. Do not be shy if you feel nervous initially. Your progress will improve if you can do it sooner. You are doomed to lose the game when your anxiety gets in the way. The bottom line is: An actor can't exist without confidence.

A second thing to remember is that confidence will help you support your decisions when it comes to your performance. It is essential to know what you are doing is right. It doesn't matter if you make it different ten more times, the director may tell you to. At least you are ahead. You rule it. Director: If you are nervous or too stressed, it is impossible to control your mind. Your perception is closed. This means that you cannot receive any instruction from them, or apply them to your acting. It is the chemistry between director/actor that brings about amazing results at the end.

Reaction and Playout

Reaction and play out are two more tools in your arsenal. These are the two ingredients that make up the actor's bread and butter. It shows presence and is always available. An actor projects emotion and receives emotion. An actor plays every day. Not just when they have something to share. They are true to themselves. They react to the situations, they react to how their partners say things, they get affected and affected by sounds, or they are affected by what their partners do. Everyone plays a role, so actors must stay focused and in the moment.

Observation

You must be able to observe all things. This should be your primary goal in life. To develop, you need stimulations. These stimulations can be taken every day. There are always people around you. People who talk every day, people who don't know you. Everybody has something that you can use. It could be your unique walking, accent, story, or even a book you've read. Or the emotion you felt in difficult times. If you are aware of how you feel, whether it is sad or happy, acting can be a fascinating way to express your feelings. These feelings should be authentic. If you aren't honest, your audience will spot it right away. You should observe everything, especially if you are experiencing something strange for the first-time. It is possible to learn from it.

Organic play - Be authentic, be in the moment

Many people succumb to the temptation of telling others certain things. It is okay to do so during the rehearsals and during the experimentation. Sometimes or most often, however, your plan doesn't work out. By that I mean it doesn't seem realistic. It's almost like you are giving a patronized performance. You'll often discover that, even though you may be trying to plan, your inner voice tells you that you are wrong. Your current situation is the reason you are wearing a wrong pattern. It's tempting to try and imitate the idea, but it isn't something that just happened. Because your partner wasn't there, nothing made you want to act or speak the way you intended. If the pace, the actor, or the condition doesn't fit what you had planned, it's likely to be bizarre and fake.

There are many ways you can say a word. There is no right and wrong. And no one can tell what you should do. You can decide to express something in a specific manner once you've made that decision. Although the director might suggest something or have a different opinion through conversations, I believe you must believe all you say. No matter how bold they may be, you must back your decision. Gerard Butler decided to try the famous "This Is Sparta" line from the movie one hundred. He tried what he saw. He believed that this was the correct way. This was the perfect match for his character. When you are clear about your intentions, what you see and think in your character's heart, the audience will too. Gerard Butler's trigger was the scene and the surrounding environment. Because Gerard Butler was emotionally hyperactive and his experiment made complete sense, as it was done organically.

Improvisation

Improvisation is a chapter all by itself. Although it existed before the concept that a script should be memorized and written, it is reasonable to not refer to this form of prototheatre as "improvised." Even though each performance was re-created from scratch.

The script gained supremacy in the theatre very quickly. Because they transfer knowledge, scripts can travel through history and last forever. They can facilitate conversations, and offer insights that can lead to new ways of translating information. The Commedia Dell'Arte, which was established in Italy in the fifteenth Century, specialized in bawdy comedies based around stock situations. They were often played by actors who had been playing them for many years. Contrary almost all theatre before it, not least from the ancient Greeks but there was no script.

Commedia Dell'Arte performers instead were allowed to freely improvise around familiar situations and dialogue exchanges. This was undoubtedly a highly successful approach that was maintained well into the eighteenth centuries. Its influence is still felt today.

Here's the basic idea of what improvisation is. It's a technique that makes you an actor. You will get many more points for your acting. Many times, it will save awkward moments like when you forget a line, your partner forgets one, or when you perform an action that feels more natural because of the moment. It is possible to improvise at a level where the audience can receive information without any problems, even if the script has not been given. Strasberg says that improvisation forces actors into thinking, acting, and speaking truthfully.

An actor without improvisation might resort to imitation and fail to complete his task. His style and truth. First, the behavior comes first, not the words. Stanislavski used spontaneity to explore the subtext of the scene's behavior without having to refer back to the script. The result was relaxed and effective actors. However, improvisation is not just used during a performance, but also as an exercise.

Improvisation is another way of discovering character. It can provide more insight and help you tap into the aspects of your characters beyond what is written in a script. This helps you become more familiar with the character you're playing. When you have the chance to improvise you can create. If you have to imagine your character doing something in the scene, even if it isn't written down, think about what they might be doing. How could they move in the scene, or interact with other people? Playfulness and fun are key to your character. Take stock. Think about how your character would relate to the space.

Listen

You may think it's obvious, but it's not. Concentrating and focusing on the details requires great energy, a lot more concentration, and very good reflexes. Once, as a director, it was my belief that actors should listen attentively even when distracted by other activities. What is that all about? What are you trying to accomplish? Acting doesn't mean acting in a certain manner. Assume you're someone else. We have just scratched the surface of how many layers this craft contains.

To listen is not to react. Listen is to pay attention and keep up the pace. Listen is to hear even your own thoughts so that you don't become boring. Listen is to be able to hear the melodies and take in the scene. Listening could also be about waiting until your partner's line ends or understanding, for instance, when they forgot something. The point of listening is to learn how you should react to any information that is heard. Mind-blowing right? It's true that we don't think about the things we do in real life. Therefore, we don't react negatively. It's our lives, and we listen to and respond 24 hours a day. If you believe that you are playing a part, then all the reactions start getting amplified. You begin to act out of realisation. It's up to you to know how to deal with it.

Our next tool is technique-Method.

In the next chapter we'll be covering some of most fundamental techniques that every actor should know. This knowledge must be mastered by every actor. These techniques are essential for performing any kind of performance that can be called organic or natural.

Chapter 12: Methodology - The Foundations Of The Acting Technique

Konstantin Stanislavski

From the moment an actor decides to become an actor, he must learn these techniques. They must learn them, be able understand them, and practice with them. What an actor uses in his work is ultimately his responsibility. If the actor is able to use the Strasberg, Meisner, or Stanislavski techniques in their work, it's his responsibility. Reality is what every actor should aim for. The ability to capture a real moment.

None of the other points are significant. Stanislavski is the one who first gave form to what we now call acting. Stanislavski uses two methods. It incorporates both physical actions as well as emotional memory. This triggers actors to act. Both are equally important. The same goes for physical actions.

Methods and Units

Stanislavski believes that every scene should be viewed as a map. Stanislavski used points of reference to help the actor create this map. They are now called objectives and units. One unit refers to a segment of a scene that contains a single main objective for an actors. The scene can have many departments and as many shifts possible. If there are multiple shifts, the objective of the scene changes. The objective should always be visible, an act. It cannot be thought as thought. It doesn't cause communication, but self-centred action. You need interaction. You must flirt with her by getting up.

Line of actions, Super objective

Super-objective refers to the ultimate goal of each character. Every scene has smaller points. All these points, when arranged together, create a set of actions the character must follow in order to achieve the super-objective. This creates the superobjective, which is the central spine, and all the objectives that lead to it. The first character might have the following objectives in order to reach this super-objective: please her, excite her, and so on.

3. Action through Analysis

This part had undergone several stages. Before we proceed to the next stage, let's first learn something that is crucial. Three questions should be asked when analysing an action. What should I do next? Why do I do it? Third, how can I do it? These three questions are posed by the character. They must be answered.

Stanislavski developed this method during his first table readings. He broke down the action into smaller parts. After realizing that actors were having difficulty distinguishing emotion from behavior, he decided to create a method. He suggested that they discuss briefly the main idea.

The next step was giving them three questions to answer during the rehearsal. This incredible tool can be used to practice improvisation as well as create dialogues directly on the spot.

4. Truth, Beliefs and the Magic If.

We mean the truth on stage, in all circumstances, is the same truth as the truth in life. The actor was trying to show the reality of truth onstage. This is because the actor doesn't believe the reality of what happens on stage, or the character they portray.

Training techniques that involve imaginative creation of events. The actor then uses magic to create their characters. What if Macbeth were me? What would you do? Actors will behave in accordance with this hypothesis. Thus, actors' choices in physical activity are determined by the character's objectives. They can stimulate this as long the actor has ample options that are both robust and true to the script.

5. Imagination

The imagination is a key component of an actor's performance and acting. A lack of imagination can lead to a huge problem on stage. It will result in a weak performance. They will show more lifelike imitations. The actor should strive to make a play look like real life using his techniques. It is here that imagination plays the largest role. It is important for actors to practice their acting skills by feeding their imagination. This will make it possible to play the role they wish to play.

6. Subtext

The audience visits the theatre to see, hear, and experience through their movements the subtext. It is the meaning underneath the dialogue. The actor interprets the subtext through intonation and gesture.

Because the plot is not yet complete, the characters and the audience share the confidential information. Without subtext, a performance is nothing but spoken words with no meanings or depth.

You can also highlight the emotion of a character in a scene by making certain physical choices. It is possible to find something deeper that defines an effort we don't even talk about. Sometimes we react unexpectedly to situations, and different emotions result in different outcomes in other people. Be specific about your choices. When your character does not speak but only hears other characters' lines in dialogue, that is a sign your character thinks. As we do in real-life. Find out what your character may think and how they react to these small movements. These small beats are what makes your character special and build his depth.

7. Motivation or the so called will

The psychic life included motivation, or 'willingness', as well as feelings and mind. The emotions of an actor were a driving force. His mind was also able to decide on physical actions. This, in turn drove the actor's will to do the specified activities.

This means that emotions are what triggered the 'will. This meant that motivation or the 'will to' was present in the subconscious from the beginning and required something to bring it out to the surface. This process automatically makes motivation important in psychological realist, which relies on subtext and hidden meanings, which an actor has to present and make the audience complicit in their actions.

8. Concentration

The actor who is able to concentrate can stay focused on his character and goals and not be distracted by the outside world, such as their audience, is a successful actor. Stanislavski used his technique to experiment with new actors about how the audience influences their performance and, consequently, their distraction. Stanislavski observed that actors are often erratic even when performing simple tasks like sitting down and taking a sip of a cup.

Because they knew they were being observed, and the audience was making them feel helpless, it was almost as if they had to learn how walk again. He was able to see concentration exercises with primarily objectives on stage or props. An actor, for example, entered the stage and had to remain focused on the object they were trying to interact with. The actor began to see the audience as not only an enemy but also a co-creator and facilitator of his performance.

9. Relaxation

To be able to control his motor and intellectual faculties, an actor has to relax. This approach can prove controversial for actors. A relaxed actor will have a reduced energy level, which could lead to poor performance. It is important to let go of all worries and to concentrate on the role we play. The body will not experience tenderness or poor performance flow if this relaxation is extended to the physical.

10. Adaptation-Subtext

Because adaptability relied on communion, each actor needed to be aware of the actions of the other actor to make adjustments.

A key function of adaptation was the ability to convey 'invisible signals' that can't be put into words. Sometimes actors with limited emotional ranges may be more efficient at transmitting subtext than actors with greater emotional ranges, but are unable to do so.

The questions of 'What' (action), 'Why (aim),' and "How" (adaptation were asked by actors in adaptation. Although it is possible to address the problems of action or aim during analysis of a play text's content, adaptation would require the actor to interact with others and make the necessary adjustments.

11. Tempo-Rhythm

To better understand Stanislavski's pattern around tempo rhythm, it is necessary to dissect the inner experience from its physical expression. Stanislavski said that Tempo is the speed at which emotion or action occurs. You could have a fast, medium or slow tempo. He divided into the Rhythm and Slow. The Internally and the Externally. Both the intensity and the external expressions of emotion were internal. Externally it was the actor's gestures, movements, and actions.

Tempo rhythms give a character great depth and richness. A solid performance is achieved when actors are able to connect physically and emotionally. Stanislavski suggested that you use music as a way to better understand this relationship with rhythm and tempo. It is obvious that a well-organized performance flows like music, when you stop and think about it.

12. The Physical Apparatus

It is possible to train the body and voice to help the actor create every action. As the body and voice of the character, his solid performance is dependent on them. The body should move with confidence and grace.

The mechanical mannerisms that are used to represent real life only add a false representation of the natural world. It is important that actors bring everything they have experienced in their daily lives to the stage. Stage must reflect the reality of daily life. The voice is just as important. The trained voice allows actors to have versatility and can work with any character. Voice is the stabilizing factor that gives every performance colour, and generates emotions.

13. Emotional Memories

Emotional Memories require that actors recreate an event from the far past in order to recreate the 'feelings' they had at the time. These emotions can be used to bring out the human depth and personal involvement of the actor in the current role. The quality and authenticity of the actor's performance is dependent on his experience and his ability draw emotions and feelings from the past.

The authentic experience was then subjected to a time filter, which changed the quality of the experience into a "poetic reflection" of life's experience. The actor is not an actor who lived a life as it was, but one that was repeated from real life. He then applied those experiences to the character and the play's current situation. The actor can generate emotion by recalling a case that has elicited similar emotions.

If the emotional reaction to the current situation is needed, it would be necessary for the actor to recall his past emotions. That was called 'Emotional Remembrance'. Through rehearsals and training, an actor developed a conditioned reaction that automatically allowed him to experience a real moment on stage. This reflex was then applied, to a specific acting condition.

Some actors may find this approach painful, especially sensitive actors. This is because emotional memories can bring out hidden situations and make it difficult to act. In order to successfully manage these emotions, an actor's teacher or director must be balanced at the beginning of his career.

Chapter 13: Lee Strasberg Method

Lee Strasberg has been called one of today's most outstanding acting teachers. He elevated Stanislavski techniques to a new level. After modifications, he designed a solid structure that includes exercises to help an actor establish his craft. Lee Strasberg believed acting doesn't stop when an actor is famous or a superstar. Acting, on the other hand, is an ongoing training program that helps the actor mature and develop.

Or he may end up copying something that's already been done. Every actor needs to bring something different to his performance. There are many Hamlets and Juliets. It does not have to be about the directing approach in a movie or play. It all comes down to the acting technique of each actor and the choices they make individually.

Most actors forget the daily training work and concentrate on the scene work. It is important that actors do thirty minutes of exercise each day. Talent alone is not enough. If you want to grow in your craft, then you must be training every day. Relaxing and concentrating are two of the most important skills in acting. To show control over yourself, you first have to settle. Next, focus on the control you have over the imaginary objects and people you want to create.

An actor can't be in full control of his or her abilities if they aren't able relax and concentrate. An actor can eliminate the mannerisms that obscure reality by engaging in relaxation and exercises. An actor brings the same habitual behavior as any human being. The unconscious repetition of behaviour is not an actor's fault. It is a result our lifestyle and conditioning. Strasberg explained that we are influenced by our culture, habits and customs.

The child is free to express everything because he doesn't have control over it. The good news is that children gradually learn to be more responsible for their actions. These behaviors and habits can cause actors to act out in ways they don't understand, or develop expressions that are not intended.

Let's now discuss the two pillars to Strasberg's technique. The sense memory as well as the emotional memory.

Sense Memory

The actor can use his five senses to react vividly to imagined objects and uses sense memory to do so. An actor can't develop further without a basic understanding memory. You can slowly seduce your senses to make them come alive as you explore objects through five senses.

Also, the senses in all people are different. This means that some senses can be stronger than others, even though the experience is the same.

By pairing sense memories with past events, we can trigger emotions. For example, the smells of freshly cut grass remind me of pre-school, and it also brings back memories about the trees in the yard. There is an emotion of happiness, freedom, and fulfillment.

Energy is not to be replaced with effort. It is quite obvious to the spectators. It is almost as if the performance has been interrupted. It is like the illusion disappears. Acting with effort means you apply mannerisms to get attention. Once you create awareness, your focus moves away from the character or partner and towards the audience. You need to push your performance harder if you don't get the reaction you desire. It can lead to everything going sideways.

Because you don't have the freedom to do what you want, stress can cause problems in everything you do. There is something you must keep in mind... There is a warning.

Emotional Memories

As we discussed in Stanislavski's technique, the emotional Memory allows us to access an experience from our past that is relevant to the situation we are currently facing. We bring it back to life and make an organic representation of the current situation. A character may want to ask a girl for his affection, but is unable to find the courage and the right words. He has an awful relationship with women. Here are some things you can do to try and recall the first time you asked a girl out. What did you feel like before you did it? What was your experience like while you were doing it. Maybe a friend had an experience like this. Keep their memories of what they felt. Once you have found the reference, take a moment to let it fill you up. Go there. Once you are feeling the same emotions again, you can begin to describe your character. You will gradually transition from the situation in the past to the current position of your character.

Chapter 14: Stanford Meisner

Meisner Technique helps you react to the behaviour of your fellow performers. Meisner Acting is based in improvisation. This is because Meisner believed that improvisation is the source that allows an actor be spontaneous and react to life moments the same as in rehearsals.

Meisner's acting is based on the ability to inhabit imaginary worlds and be someone else. These exercises train actors' observation and alertness, and help them step into the new worlds.

Repetition Exercise

Two actors are asked to stand in front of each other, making observations and repeating the comments. You need to be relaxed, concentrated, and to remain focused. Meisner exercises all require an additional actor. To make the activities more interesting, I recommend taking someone you're familiar with. This is an example:

The first actor says

1: Your right limb is moving

The other one states:

2: My right thigh is moving

3: Your right limb is moving

4: Yes, I can feel my right leg moving

5: Your right limb is moving

6: My right thigh is moving

7: Your right thigh is moving

8: Yes, I can feel my right leg moving

The ultimate goal here is to forget about the text and focus more on our interactions and each other's gestures and behaviours. Meisner refers this to the "reality is doing". This can lead to new meanings in your performances as a duo by learning how to respond in scene to your partner.

Meisner techniques require that actors do not learn lines through intonations. They need to maintain the element of surprise. As if they just heard it for the first time and are able to produce the right line spontaneously. Because the moment triggers all the reactions, it gives rise to a real performance.

REPETITION

The Objective Repetition, without modifications

It begins with one person commenting about the first thing they notice in their partner acting, followed by another repeating what they said. The same observation is repeated over and over again. It is a simple but effective exercise that teaches actors how they can honor their instincts.

Meisner's technique relies on you stopping judging what you see. If you first notice that your nose is large, it's time to tell the truth! The ability to react with your heart and not your brain is what you learn. You can also stop trying to create new words or ideas by simply repeating. This allows you to act instead of thinking.

To be able read the behavior of your partner, you must focus your attention on one thing. The ability to stay focused is vital when we become distracted by outside factors. The ultimate goal of being present with others and not getting distracted by irrelevant information is to be present. The ability to concentrate on something other than yourself is a great way to calm nerves before and during performances, as well as in everyday life.

It is how much you allow yourself to feel affected by others, and how your body and voice react to affection. You make it clear. We were taught as children not to show vulnerability or weakness because it can create tension. Tension stops an actor being expressive. It locks all his sensations and his movements. Tension is the greatest enemy as it locks the mind, body and soul.

Bottom line: In real life we are taught to present the best of ourselves. For example, see how you act when meeting someone of importance for the first-time. But, as actors, you must be trained to only show your true self.

At first it can make you look robotic and unnatural. You are trapped by fear of not being able to do the job right. You must get rid the idea that you have the right answer and make sure you inflate yourself with the affirmation you need.

Repetition with adjustments

You can alter the repetition if your partner urges you to. It might be as simple a "you moved your right eye", or something more complicated like "you are flirting." It doesn't matter what you notice at the beginning. You can translate it later. If you cannot express what you see, it is easier to repeat what you already said. This prevents you from trying to find the best way to continue your previous line. Instead, try something more interesting about what was next.

Remember to be consistent, not intellectualize. This stage helps an actor to recognize behaviour and calls it without polite editing. This step will increase your instinct and help you stay focused on your observation. The repetition exercise allows you to control the changes. However, this means that you can still use your senses, instincts, observation, intuition, and brain to make an assessment of how the actor is acting.

Chapter 15: Michael Chekhov

Imagination

Chekhov invented a technique for acting and performing that, unlike Stanislavski's emotional recall, was based upon imagination and movement. His innovative approach to creativity and imagery was unlike anything ever taught.

He mentioned image work. The actor was instructed to use his imagination to create an image and then let it grow and change, before finally adopting it during the performance. Chekhov was determined bring the vision back to its original place of importance. Stanislavski had forgotten it.

Stanislavski Chekhov

Emotional Memory Personal Imagination

To stimulate feeling

Chekhov said that the actor shouldn't be limited in using his personal and emotional memories of his life to help him understand

and create a character. He cannot only use imagination as a way to stimulate emotions. However, he will never be deprived of his personal experience and he will not be affected as much if he uses resources from his own past experiences. He would soon be without his references. Stanislavski said the opposite. He believes that as long an actor is attentive to those around him, it will be impossible for him to lose connections. The more he watches, he gains experience and memories that he can use in the production of a play.

Each technique is based on daily practice that an actor does to sharpen his craft. To keep your instincts sharp, you need to practice every single day. You can use your imagination to help you train on a certain topic every day. If you put him under certain conditions, it will become second nature. This gives you immediate access, rather than emotional recall, to a tool that can provide stimulus.

Qualities

Chekhov used this word to replace emotion. He knows that asking for a feeling straight is the best way make it run away. Instead of saying "be more happy here", try adding a quality of joy to what you do. Students are asked to find personal motivation rather than to cause despair by adding the quality of anger to their gestures and movements.

This method was helpful when we were working on monologues during drama school. Sometimes it was beneficial to point out the qualities prior to the monologue's performance. Other people were also present during the performance. For example, while I was performing the monologue I was also taking notes to help me implement them. It is a wonderful practice that improves alertness, and helps you draw out emotions on the spot.

Chekhov called his work "psychophysical@ as interfering with your imagined body can result in psychological and physical changes.

The Psychological Gesture

Psychology is activated through movement. Actors can act organically toward a situation when their minds are directed. This helps to build the character. A psychological gesture is an expression of the character's thinking and actions. They could be as small as a gesture of a finger or as large as a silent movement and an exhale at their end.

I will give you an illustration.

Prada Meryl Straep, the character of Devil wears, makes certain movements with her glasses. The way she holds her glasses, the way they are taken off, the way in which she watches people from head to foot, and the way she turns the page on a newspaper. All these gestures show character. The subtext can be enlightened through psychological motions in other worlds.

A performer would benefit from a rich source of inspiration by consciously working the gestures. The psychological gesture technique seeks to bring out the emotions through the intuitive sense. This feeling is essential for good acting.

When such a gesture is associated with a defined action or objective, make it visible at home in the most obvious way. Once you've done the gesture several time, start saying the lines as you go. Now imagine you are driving it inwardly. You will feel the motion in your work and it will serve as an inspiration for your next action or objective. It will help to connect your body and brain.

The Chart to Inspire Acting

Chekhov designed a Chart for Inspired Acting. This chart was created to explain his technique. This chart included the previously mentioned concepts, qualities, psychological gesticulations, imagination, and other key elements of the technique. Chekhov's technique involves more than imagination and mental gestures. They have been highlighted as important elements and illustrations of the differences between Stanislavski's technique.

ENERGY

Nothing can be effective without energy. Natural energy is unlimited... The human body acts as a conduit for natural energy. Each organ of our bodies requires energy to function. The energy that we have is the same as our body. Without energy, there is no performance. The actor need not be hyperactive to perform well. However, energy can also refer to being aware and able to control their body's movements.

IMAGINATION

When our minds are filled with energy, we call it imagination. Energy, as we have already said, is the key. It is the fuel that drives your acting. It is essential to continue our acting training and improve our craft. It is essential for Chekhov acting. To learn and follow this method, every student-actor must have an imagination. We are actors. When we act, we create a fictional line and move into another realm, becoming someone else. You still have the same abilities in reality, but you can use them in another universe. One more literal. You need to feel the sensations that trigger your imagination.

CONCENTRATION

Concentration is essential for any activity that has great potential to achieve success.

Focusing does not mean that you can think more clearly.

When you focus, you can send your attention towards an object. If you become one of the pictures, you will feel its Quality, sense its personality and get impressions and impulses. A concentrated artist has the ability to influence and manipulate his audience with his performance.

Without concentration, art is impossible to create. The audience is attracted to a well-done performance and will move toward it. It is an exciting journey for them. The actor attracts their pleasant sensation.

Focusing on the character that he has imagined will help an artist transfer his values to the audience. This is a preview about an element of Chekhov's technique.

INCORPORATION

Acting can be expressed and incorporated into our bodies. Your imagination can capture the details of the character and the goals he must achieve. This is how the body defines and radiates the image. The body is like an instrument. It plays the notes. Acting is a complete act of the body. Concentration is the direct cause of incorporation.

RADIATION

The inner secrets that are necessary to act, such as knowledge, feelings, and actions, must be revealed in the final performance. To make them feel sorry for the heroes. You must convey the emotion that will shock the audience.

The actor must radiate in every performance of acting. He wants to draw the audience along with him. The audience needs to know what the actor is trying to communicate to them. He communicates to the audience his character's goals. This action succeeds when the actor feels it. As a result, he is satisfied with the outcome and the audience, who are witnesses of the impact, feel enchanted and content.

DIRECTION Is A FORCE

Movement is confined to a space. Usually, it happens in one direction. Six directions feel like absolute force.

These directions are dynamic:

A)Expanding or contracting

B)forward and reverse

C) Up and down.

They are closely connected to all sensations and all the activities actors take part. It is the foundation of the performance.

FOCAL POINTS

The information they provide for us and others is not relevant to the scene. These focal points must be found by the actor in his readings of a play or script. He must also know what moments are most important to his character. Then, his job is to direct the audience towards these points during the performance.

It is up to him to decide how to convey the information. This is what defines him, as an artist. It can be a moment of silence. It could also be a gesture. One thing is certain. It should be simple enough for the audience to grasp, but not too complicated for the partner.

ENSEMBLE

Theatre is a collective art. Many artists create scenes and imagine worlds together, inviting the audience to come along. Does it take a collective effort to create something believable and enchant the audience?

ATMOSPHERES

When we refer to atmospheres, we don't mean what the environment is that allows for the action to take place. It also refers to the personal environment that each character enjoys. A character who has experienced many things and has overcome many difficulties brings something with him.

He is carrying heavy energy. All the signals we receive to communicate the message. This is called the creation of an environment. You might get bad news if somebody comes to your home. He will bring with himself an atmosphere. He will create an atmosphere that supports this. Because they determine our personalities, atmospheric factors are crucial.

QUALITY

How we respond to different circumstances is a reflection of the quality. Quality can transform one thing to many other things. It can make a joke into a kiss, or a seduction into the end. Quality is how an act is performed by another. The actor feels the quality directly. It is what gives them the most joy when portraying a character different from themselves. It is their Ethos.

For character descriptions, we often use words like strong, tender, confident, proud and heavy. There are many qualities that can be used to describe our inner and outer movements. These will have a unique meaning depending on how they are performed. If they are able to show something. If they show something. The best part of this technique is the fact that you can travel outside to source materials for your creations. We can see the beauty in the world around and appreciate it creatively. It is possible to see the pace of objects, images, people. It is possible to perceive something authentic about objects, images and people. You can feel a connection for them.

THINKING. FEELING. Willing.

These three functions represent the simplest of all human activities. They are so natural that we use them in our performances as actors. Because these functions often conceal the deepest complexities and nuances of a character. It is up to you to discover them.

We are able to think. It is our domain. We can also feel and often our thoughts cause our feelings. Action, doing, and expressions are the functions of will power. This view is not comprehensive, but it includes all possible options.

These functions serve as beautiful containers for putting the play's material in the characters around each other, the words and expressions they use, or hearing them.

Chekhov suggested that a better way to understand these three pillars is to look at a play like a living person. Every play has ideas, atmospheres tensions conflicts, tensions, and they all create feelings. Therefore, the characters can act on them. These real things can be seen and experienced by the audience.

Thinking is something we all already do so it's not necessary to stop thinking. It's not work, it's just clarifying the character's intentions or showing his mannerisms that show what he thinks.

As an example, when we see a chair we don't understand why it has four legs. It is just the way it is. At first glance, it seems stable. This is a piece we don't need to think about. It is necessary to think about how we can break it down into smaller pieces. You need to think about how to balance it on three legs, with the same stability that allows you to create an innovation on a different level. They will be clear to the audience. Thinking is reflected in actions.

Love can heal broken hearts in all languages. Though we do not think with the hearts of our bodies, with a literal type of talk, it is possible to speak from and listen to their hearts. It is something that poets have used numerous times.

A FEELING DISASTER

This is when someone performs well on a task. It's also obvious when there is lack of comfort. The more dangerous the action, the greater the challenge for the actor. However, it's not as easy as making it look easy. Because the audience doesn't want to worry about actors on the stage in the same way they worry about characters, or at least not to the same degree.

Actors must know the details of every choreography if sword fighting is to be performed on stage. You must have grace and keep your cool, even if you are fighting the hardest fights. The audience will pay more attention to the actors than the actors if they can fight correctly.

The illusion should be convincing enough that the audience doesn't think about anything but the action.

A FEELING of Form

The human body is a form. Every day we feel it. Since our childhoods, we strive to understand its potential and make good use of it. The feeling of form doesn't just depend on how it feels after an injury, illness, anxiety or other circumstances. As a whole, you need to look at the body as a whole. You feel every single part. To walk on various surfaces. The essence of what comes later. In order to fully comprehend how you can revive it, you must create a starting, middle, and ending.

You can feel the beauty in your skin

This element is complicated and holds many valuable values. All animals have beauty, grace and they are all faithful and honest with themselves. They act as they are meant to and do not hide anything or try to impress others. Flowers have this beauty, even though they only exist to be beautiful to the eyes.

Everything goes wrong when you try to make yourself beautiful by making extra efforts. The beauty of the truth is gone when you are unable to use your energy or have physical storage.

A feeling that is all-encompassing

An actor should understand that acting is not a one-man show. It's about working together as a team. Even though an actor may not be present in every scene, he is still part of the larger team.

To make this clear, an amazing exercise trains actors' perceptions and helps them to understand the whole. For it to work well, you have to be at minimum 8 actors. Make sure you have enough space. This stage can be described as a tray that balances on top of the giant ball. It is your job to make this tray balance. As such, you must continue moving across the surface, changing directions as needed and filling any gaps left by others. You don't need to be able to visualize where you are going. Be aware. Change directions suddenly. Be unpredictable. After a while you'll see that all the actors will be well orchestrated together, and you won't even be falling upon one another.

Chapter 16: You Can Find Your Own Way

After years of hard work and practice, you will begin to see the automated techniques you have used in your acting. The actor adds his personality and mechanisms to the techniques so that he creates something original that works for him. Acting can be a difficult craft. There will always be something to learn.

Our heroes are the famous actors who can't explain what acting is. But they keep trying. Even though they are able to work after so many years, they still try to discover something new and different. These techniques are the key to understanding why it doesn't matter. They are the map. To get to your destination, you must still drive. It doesn't matter what technique you use. What matters is that it works well for you, and what gets you the acceptance of others.

Chapter 17: Reading From The Table

You are now familiar with the tools actors need, and have been introduced some of the most popular acting techniques. These tools will help you be more precise with your acting and make more sense. This is how an actor should begin reading a script.

The magic of table reading is where it all begins. Actors must prepare for rehearsals by being ready to hit particular marks during reading. Table Reading and Rehearsals, which are often performed in the theatre, can be very beneficial. Explore your voice. You aren't stabilizing anything while you read.

Your character is not your friend, and you don't even know what his emotions are or how the story will unfold. You will now try to determine how the character will sound. Try new ways and don't be afraid. Don't be afraid to get out of the comfort zone and do something new. It is not a good idea to be embarrassed about an act you attempt. Period. You shouldn't attempt to project emotion during the first three reads. You can start by reading the book in a introductory way and seeing how it moves you. The pace will then follow. You should not ignore the punctuation between the lines.

You must use punctuation to make sure you understand the structure of what is being read. However, it's another story when it comes to the actual speaking of it. Find rhythms. You can speed up, slow down or do anything you like. There is no right or wrong way to do things. It is fun to experiment with different ways to express a single line. Let the moment be your guide. As we speak, listen attentively. This is another thing that can affect the way we speak. Reacting means acting.

Another key point to remember, as we already said, is to try not fixing lines that aren't related to the table reading. This will only make you appear fake. You might have an idea about what you want. Fine. Or to use a phrase in a particular way you've imagined. Fantastic. But. You don't have the ability to remember the lines and you haven't acted yet. These two elements will overtake whatever you set down at a table while you sat on a stool reading.

While you're reading the table, focus simultaneously on the character aspects. Mark down the details that will help your understanding of him. Get to know his intentions. While we will cover this in greater detail in the chapter regarding building the character, it is important that you start to observe his intentions. It is necessary to underline the fact that you are portraying a cop who violates the law. This is something you must understand. Research is the final thing. Once you have read through the story and heard your character speak, you can now dive deeper into the details.

You might notice a difference in your accent depending on where the story takes place. What genre is this? It can be sci-fi. Westerns. War movies. Drama. Comedy. Find the best aspects of your character within this environment. Like we said, if he is a detective, it is important to find out more about the job and what you should do. It is important to research for every role, and actors do this if they are interested in the truth and significant depths of their characters.

Chapter 18: The Secrets To A Successful Rehearsal

Rehearsals are the key stage in any actor's preparation. Although rehearsal is an essential part of acting, most actors are not able to do it in the same timeframe as TV or films. Rehearsing is crucial for theatre. It is vital to a successful play and the development of characters.

After reading the lines, the actors slowly stand up. Although it is always better to know the lines by this time, it is still better. So you get up, regardless of whether the lines are on your hands or not. Then you move on, going with your gut and intuition. Once you feel like you are a character, then you can start to put it into practice.

You can think and act like the character that you play from the moment rehearsal begins. When you think like your character, you can discover many things around your performance. Let's examine a scene in rehearsal. Drama schools give two actors a piece to play for almost the whole year. They have the opportunity to learn inside this piece and the play.

This will allow the actor to learn more about his collaborators, and how they come together in mutual agreements. You can't do anything wrong. Everything is part of the creative process. Your tutor-director is responsible for fixing and/or completely changing anything. Some actors will criticize themselves during rehearsals from the very beginning. They believe they aren't good enough, or their actions aren't being projected to the audience.

This is normal. But once you notice it, you will remove it. It stops you from being free and completely unaffected. Don't make assumptions about yourself. You are responsible for finding the character. Do the best you can and just show it. Spread your thoughts. Even exaggerating at times. The tutor-directors' job is to give the piece quality shape and clear it of all its imperfections. You will then be able to run the entire piece with your partner a few more times. Next, analyse it by identifying the key points and moments that will make the piece thrilling and memorable.

Even though it can be difficult in a short scene to show certain elements of a person, you should still read the play and try to create the character as if they were part of the whole story. The result is a complete character who jumps in to the scene. At some point you will be exposed to director's ideas. His vision of the piece. Some ideas may not match your vision. Ask questions when you are on the stage at a drama school.

It's not clear why this or that should be done. Talking about it is always possible. A tutor may have more experience than you do and can see the details better than you. However, it is important to be able to discuss your ideas and plan for this scene. Your rehearsal also includes a unique method of running through the lines, without actually performing what you will be performing, but with different improvisations.

If you say, for example. I am going to stay home because I'm tired. It's possible to say this line sitting on the couch. The remote control will allow you to change channels and read a book. Once you are done, get up and scrub the floor. Because the effort is different.

Here is another tip which will help you with the memorization line. Stand close to a wall. About an inch. You can speak up about any of your lines. All your lines. They don't have to be arranged in a particular order. Concentrate on your voice. Use different voices and tones to create depth. Take the simple fact that you can hear your lines echo back to you. Then, simultaneously try and find the voice of the character. Your lines create an automatic mechanism for memorization.

Chapter 19: Preparing A Monologue In Theatre

This is my favorite chapter. Because you must prepare a monologue for the acting initiation. For your audition at drama school, you will need to prepare a monologue. Also, a monologue is required for auditions in a theatrical production. It is the moment after years of waiting and dreaming. It's the moment you can finally do it.

You may experience some unpleasant things during your initiation. It is okay. They are an artistic process. It is important to accept mistakes and exaggerations as they will help you grow. You can see the raw emotion and emotions when you begin a monologue.

I realized that the monologue was taking control of me and that I was losing my ability to perform it. I was losing control. The monologue was bursting with anger and I couldn't control it. The monologue's goal was not met, so the lines were incorrect and the performance was poor. Although the first attempts were disastrous, it was so much fun and I learned so much from this procedure. This allows you to gain valuable experience before you work with others on a scene.

Every day, I was looking for ways to improve my mistakes and sat down with my tutor notes. They were my best friend and helped me understand what I was doing. You need to be patient with yourself, and you must understand the process. Exposure. The way you stand, talk, and move. All things must be your focus. To be a successful performer, you must change any bad habits that you may have. It is not possible to walk with your feet dragging because it is what you are used too. Only take on the role when it is required.

Your goal is to keep the energy up and manageable while keeping your audience's attention on you. The attention of your audience is solely on you. There's nothing that could distract them.

It is possible to break down the monologue in sections.

Before you can begin working on a monologue from a play, you must first read it. To fully understand your character, you must get into his head. You will be able to comprehend what you are dealing. These elements will help you understand the purpose of creating monologues.

Even though you have the ability to make changes later, it is impossible to stop practicing. Everything is literary. At first, you will need to work on your monologue in accordance with the intended paths. After the reading is complete, you can take the monologue. Then you need to break it up into smaller sections. We do this to make it easier for the audience to understand what we are saying. This is so that the audience understands our message first.

We also said that you do not take into account the punctuation during monologues. In performing, you don't care about commas.

Sometimes you will need pace purposes in order to unite meanings within one rhythm.

This is marked by a small tilde. The tilde reminds to keep up the beat. We also have to mention that during this process, we try and find elements that relate to the character being portrayed. The time you have to showcase what you've got in a monologue is usually less than two minutes. It is even more important to audition. The key to finding the character is knowing what's going to happen before and after. That's why we read the whole book. Be truthful and don't let anyone stare at you for more than two minutes.

Find the main points

You can now start working differently after you have completed the breakdown. You will find the key points in the monologue. The parts where you create something substantive will be found. It will be a major shift in the landscape. Understanding the main points helps you to comprehend the main objectives of our character in this monologue. He wants to make an argument.

This statement must be precise. These are the key points that will be highlighted in any monologue. Otherwise, the monologue would be dull and boring. Sometimes the main objectives can be a chance to do something different. Hamlet begins his monologue with the famous "To be or not to" line. This line has been recited millions of times. It has been performed many times by talented actors. It has been mocked and used in comedy. You won't have to stress this part if you are trying to play this.

If an actor wants to make a mark with monologues, he must also include a suggestion. This is something that has never been done before. It is not easy, I know. It is. However, this is a foundation that must be built. At the end of the day, all we really mean by honesty in everything we do is to give it our best. That's what will make it distinctive and certainly unique. We are all unique.

The following monologue is in addition to the play Pillowman by Martin McDonagh

Ariel is a police officer.

We use symbols for the rhythm and pace areas that we have mentioned: slash/double slash/tilde/arrow to highlight something.

Highlight the meanings that are lost.

Subtext refers to the text between the parenthesis

So, let me tell you all about me.//

(Let me be honest, I'm not going to let you fuck me.

There is an overwhelming!

(So, basically, if it was different, I'd already have your neck in the palm of my hand. I don't like you and never will. People like this shouldn't exist. You want to know why I do what I do?

People who even put the smallest of fingers on children --

(In my view, it is wrong for anyone to even touch a child. You sick bastards, this is my reason.

It wakes up with me.

(What you have done haunts. I can't go to sleep. I don't know what kind of people would have done this. But you still have the gut to look at it. You think I'm just another cop. You think I'd rather work in an office than out on the fields? It's not fair.

I always arrive on time. I am punctual and make sure the bindings are clean.

(My life has been surrounded by adrenaline. I feel the need to burrow people like you. But I want people who like me to know that I am a pain. I'm always there.

Sometimes, I use excessive force. I sometimes use excessive force to inflict injury on innocent people.

(Sometimes I get carried away, but there's a reason. There's always a reason. If you think that I enjoy hurting someone else, you might be right. But only when they merit it. People like you deserve it all. So I don't feel guilty)

/

(I'm aware that excessive force is against the law. But, what are you going? Are you going to snitch on me? This gives me an additional reason to use excessive force to get my mouth shut once and for all. This is how terrible it can get.

You know what? But I don't care./ "Cos when they resent me,!" you know? !Little children will follow my around!, and I'm sure they'll remember my name and what my stand for! and I'll be giving them some sweets as thanks!

I have a goal. This dream gives me balance and helps me forget all of my worries, even if it's not what I want. Deep within, I realize that I am not a bad individual. I just need to live in a better community. Safe. Without you, it would be unsafe. So, when I grow up, I'll be satisfied that I did my job and served well.

Background stories can be used to stimulate your imagination.

You can trick your brain with fake stimulation to make an emotion or trigger your thought. This fake stimulation will cause real emotions to be generated. Let's consider an example. Imagine that you are playing a character with no income, but who is having financial difficulties.

He is a salesman for another person's profit. He studies in a school that does not have a regular schedule and dreams of changing his life. This is your information. Now you need to connect with him. You are in a position where you've never been before and need to sell. This is a man who lives in poverty. He was born on the streets and his parents abandoned him as they couldn't provide for him.

Start with a simple thought. Imagine what it would be like if you had no other possession than a keychain. You can think of something you loved as child and would do anything to have it. Perhaps there was a moment in your past where you had to go to an interview. You would have to pass it or you would lose your job. It is possible to get this idea into your head and make it a reality by working around it. You must achieve something regardless of the obstacles. You don't consider the obstacles. You are only focused on the goal.

It is my goal to win the interview. I must see as many chains I can because I'm going have to feed my family. Next came the second step. The second step is to instill the fear of not succeeding. The consequences of this outcome will be shocking. Next, start to improvise. You'll see significant changes in your facial expressions as well as your mood. However, the key is to believe every word you say and to be open with your references.

Finalize your script by applying all of these concepts to every line. This will create real situations that you can use to make yourself real.

Attracting the eye through posture and movement

Movement and posture are two of the most important tools an actor has when performing on stage. Both of these give him the ability provide clarity, strength, presence and authority to his characters. However, these qualities are essential to maintain the interest of the audience. Before we begin the monologue, we draw, or as I like to call it, the movement and posture. You will see how your character moves and what he stands.

I want to emphasise something that is really, truly important. It is vital to be able to act. Energy. Without energy, you will be just someone who writes a lot of words on paper. Energy is everything. Get enough energy before you start working. You must always be focused and in control. It is crucial. This does not mean that all energy is exaggerated. Your presence is essential. You are a mark. A statement can be anything you say.

Everything is simple. Let's move on to the drawing. You want attention. This is why you need to create something that works. You could take for example. As if you were to play Richard the third by William Shakespeare. So everyone knows that King Richard has mild limping and scoliosis. This is the first thing to do. If you do it well, everyone will notice you.

Monologue setting

The monologue is difficult because you can't show too much in the short time, but you also need to have clear intentions. First, you have to choose whether to use props. Many actors use a stool as a prop. It doesn't matter whether they will use it for their first act or the last. It is not worth it to try to make it work if you don't want to be there.

It will make you look awkward, and it will show that your weakness is that of being unable to stand. Be sure to use whatever you have. Four moments are essential to make your monologue entertaining and effective. Of course, this is the beginning. How does it begin? It is important to take a few moments to slow down and exhale before you begin. Relax, feel confident, and be ready to give your best. All you have to think about are the marks you need.

Once they do that, you start charging them. There is no need to do more than necessary. Do not attempt to create unnecessary movements in order to fill in any gaps. If it isn't natural to move, don't. Sitting in a chair doesn't make your monologue any more powerful. All that matters is to keep control. Here's another important tip: Keep your body under control at ALL times. Many new actors have problems with their hands.

This is because you lack energy and confidence. Your hands will find their way when you are focused and understand every word. Be relaxed even if you're standing in one place. The body will shift the weight of stressed people to one side. It doesn't seem right. It's almost as if you are out of balance. This can definitely impact your ability and performance. It is important to first learn how stand well, with a strong appearance, and then to walk.

You'll be exposed. Once you have this down, you can start to create the core of the monologue. The last tip is to always start with your intended intention. Change your focus and you'll lose strength.

Use the emotion

After a catchy, impressive beginning, you can start to lift the emotions. It is important to have a general understanding of the monologue. That is possible with the rule that three acts works. The rule of three acts is the beginning, middle and end. The middle could be described as your build-up. You build up tension. Here you must focus on your character, and how he feels at any given moment. But... Be unpredictable. Your actor qualities must be shown in the monologue.

This is a must. Without it, your monologue could become another one. Don't make eye contact when you address. Don't look directly at the judge or director. If you look at them, it might make them feel uncomfortable. This could cause them to stop doing what they are doing. When setting up your set-up, make sure you face your audience at all times.

If necessary, you can turn your head if you must. Of course, you will turn your back if necessary. Plus, it is risky and fascinating to do so. However, in theatre, all of our bodies are exposed to the audience. So, everything we do matters. It's not like in a movie where you know exactly when you are at that moment. So you don't really care about what your body does.

Everything has a reason and a place in theatre. The rhythm can also be shifted as a hint during the buildup. The rhythm is an integral component of an actor's performance. Without rhythm, the actor may become dull and without any interest. It is essential that the performance conveys a sense of musicality and creates emotion. It is important to pay attention to these details.

Reaching the summit of the monologue

At some point it must become obvious that you are approaching a peak. It doesn't matter if your comedy or drama is funny, you have to do this. This is your moment. This moment is when you must achieve the highest level of emotional performance.

I want to suggest something. As an exercise, I suggest that you work on a monologue daily. You can dedicate 15 minutes of your time each day to this exercise. This will ensure that you are always ready and able to tackle any material that may come up later in auditions. Each month, you can change the monologue and do the same thing again.

Also, you can change your gender. You can imagine how much work it will take and how many plays this year. Use every day to learn and improve your craft. Don't be afraid to take risks with your performance. You never know what you might get and how it will work out. Anything you can imagine is possible. You will feel more confident and will therefore have more energy.

Begin to learn the craft of acting now. Experienced eyes will help you understand how to perform monologues. When you have done many monologues and are familiar with the rules, it will be easy to put together a monologue. You will then be prepared for an audition.

How to choose a monologue that is good

* Take a chance on something that you initially feel a connection to. If you feel confident writing for yourself, I encourage it. You will be able to better understand yourself and your own needs. There is no one better than you. You are able to better understand yourself and your personal preferences.

* If you are choosing an existing one you need to fully comprehend the context. Which part of the world are you in? What time is this?

Who are they? And, most importantly, to whom are you speaking?

* You must set clear goals. Always raise the stakes

* Never choose pieces that exceed 2 minutes. It will be more intense and concise.

* Remember to keep the three acts in order. Your monologue must have an opening, middle, and ending.

Chapter 20: Acting Tips For Drama Schools

This section is an extra section I created to offer you additional tips about the day you audition at a drama academy. Naturally, stress is a result of this process. You must fight to reverse this process in your favor. It is important to remember that if you change it in your favor, then you will get energy and confidence. The audition is upon us.

Whatever time the audition is at, you will get up early the next day. You shower, have your breakfast and get ready for the day. Put your head against the wall and try to focus on the tasks you were called to accomplish that day. Which goals do you need to achieve? From the beginning of who you are to the end, your monologue will be a reflection of who you really are. Remember that a smile is key to an audition. This relaxes you and lets the judges know that they have someone in charge. You should only speak what is necessary.

Keep it short and professional. When you're done with your meditation, get ready to go.

It's best to be there at least an hour ahead of time. This will give your body time to warm up, and your voice can be used to help you get in touch with your inner self. Once you've finished your slate and answered the questions, it might be time to start your monologue. We said that it takes a few minutes. Focus on the character and what it is you are about.

Keep your lines straight and don't change. Your emotional depths should be plumbed and you should have an arc. You need to know where you are, where your came from and where it will lead you. Enunciate. You shouldn't be tempted to improvise unless asked. Do not wear costume, but be sure to look the part. Prepare a detailed plan of your character before you arrive at auditions.

You want everyone to be with you as you travel through the scene. You must make every impression. Remember that acting is an art form. You must make people look at you. Be your best self. Sometimes, auditions don't reflect your performance. The director might not want you to have the right look. Not everyone is right for you. You don't have to dwell on what parts you don't get.

Preparing a monologue in audition tape for a feature

Film monologue preparation is more difficult than theatre because we are relegated to the middle of the head. The options are very limited from the beginning. The things we're going to set up. That's why we don't care. However, there are three important factors we must focus on if we want something to succeed.

The actor may have difficulty being truthful in his first performances if he has become used to the process of preparing monologues for the theatre. This can be because the actor is performing close-up moves and expressions, much like he does in the theater, so everything has to be bigger for the audience to be able to see them. This can cause problems in the performances. It's because he appears to be exaggerating and doesn't believe any of the statements he makes.

It would be wonderful if the actor could do the same in the theatre. But, for the screen it isn't possible. You might have heard that an actor in these close-ups must completely forget about the camera and speak the words naturally. It's common for actors to try out many different things at once. You can't play the monologue you created for theatre if you don't do enough. The others will only see an exaggerated performance of your monologue, with intense expressions, and excessive head movements. Most likely, your voice will be much louder than it is necessary.

Even if you just want to tell the story, it is possible. Go through the monologue several times before starting the monologue. Next, you will need to reread the play, or the entire script, if possible. Then you'll have a full understanding of what has been going on in the past and future. Continue reading the chapter and then break down the monologue.

After you've done the exact same thing, you can decide whether you want to sit or stand. Both shots will use the same crop. Your face must be the focus of all monologues for the screen.

Maybe it'll be your expression, perhaps a glance. The best way to discover voices, improve your speaking ability, and speak naturally is to practice monologues. To learn how to use subtext. What happens beneath the lines? This applies to all acting. You can do this in theatre, film, or television. The movie may have scenes with no dialogue or the listener might be in them.

This subtext is what you will need to fill in. Somewhere in your head is something. The inner lines must be spoken. You can use the internal lines to help you communicate the actual lines. It is possible to find powerful ideas when you examine and mark the primary objectives that we have discussed. It will also take extra effort to make the whole thing work.

Splitting the monologue in sections allows you to stabilize your intentions as characters. Then your mood changes according to the circumstances. This is also a clarification. If we choose points where we intend to change our intentions, that doesn't mean we have to drastically change it to make it look strange.

You are aware that there is a change. Build it slowly, and unleash it when it's time. If you make your technique visible to the crowd, you'll lose the game. It is not acting. It's not possible to convince.

Drawing attention to your face

We never look in the lenses. We always look slightly to one side. You choose which side. Most of the times, you are on your right. On the side, you can imagine the person to whom you address the monologue. Keep an eye out for big head turns. The same as you would in the theatre. They should be extremely small and smooth. The total focus must be in your eyes. Stability makes your eyes more dynamic. All you need to do is focus.

The pace and beats

In this chapter I will once again mention the importance and value of pace. The monologue's impact will be even more evident if you can control your inner rhythm and energy. The technical aspect of this is that once you master breathing and speaking from the diaphragm you will be able to let more air into the film.

The reason is that you are less vocal in your project. You don't necessarily have to shout from the top like you do in the theatre. This extra tool will allow you to perform with a better intonation, faster speeds, beautiful, vibrant voices, and spoken meanings not possible in theatre.

Audition Tape

I wanted the chance to say a few words about the audition tape. Auditions tapes should be a regular part of an actor's routine. These are some tips to help you deliver a professional performance on any aspect tape. First, there is a positive aspect to the video. You can do as many takes until you get the look you desire. Not necessarily.

If you plan to take one after another, it won't be easy to choose the one that has the greatest impact and is the most effective. You'll end up with at the very least five final shots, and they will all look identical.

If not, it will not be a significant one. This will be an alternative suggestion to the casting directors. It will make them smile and say, "I didn't expect that." Send them at least two takes. You can send them one take that is very close to the information you have received or understand by reading through the scene. Or, you can send them another suggestion. The suggestion should be unique from the beginning to end.

You don't necessarily have to choose one moment to make something unique in a scene. You need to make almost the character you want. This will help you see the character from a different perspective. Practice a lot before you begin self-taping. You will need only three takes after you have successfully melted the lines.

Only two things can make you do more: you either messed it up at a bar or you forgot something. Don't try to do more than what you did in your first performance. Or, as we have said, only one take.

A reminder to you that it is important to warm up your vocal chords using the techniques and also to warm up your mask. Let's look at the technical aspect of the monologue. Many actors use their phones for audition tapes. Your phone should be able to provide high-quality video.

Pay attention the lights. The lights must be bright. You have two options. A softbox or a ringlight. Both do a great job. It is important to have bright light and no shadows around your face or behind you. They can distract. A plain background is also important. You should not have any objects or other distractions around you. Sound. Sound is another crucial element. Your phone should do a good job. You might consider purchasing an external microphone. It will give you clear sound and allow you to communicate clearly without having to be bothered.

Before you begin your audition tape you need to create a 15-30-minute ritual that grounds, engages and grounds you. One example is to read something inspiring and uplifting. Another option is to meditate, stretch or take a walk outside. Then, come back. You need something to energize and focus your attention at the same moment. Use your creativity to find the right combination of things. You must dedicate time every single day. Even if there is no acting gig, you need to keep learning. You will be able to get the most useful information and reactions faster if you have sharper mental faculties. An intelligent actor is a solid actor.

Write down five to ten activities that stimulate your brain. Perhaps you enjoy reading a book. Maybe it's classical music.

Music is one of my favorite things to listen to. They trigger my imagination to create imaginary worlds and characters. It gives me a clear mind and helps me organize the information that I need. You can find these activities to help you focus on what was said in your audition tape.

Chapter 21: Acting Fundamentals

Given Circumstances, the made-up world, the physical and social environment

Relationships- What you do with everything and everyone around.

Objective- what your character needs, desires or hopes for.

Obstacle- Any obstacle that stands in the way of our character's goals.

Strategy can either be an instinctive or deliberate plan to get the results you desire.

Tactics: The steps required to execute the character's strategy.

Evaluation- An evaluation is when an impulse is contained and multiple options are considered.

Subtext: What you mean rather than what you say.

Beat- When you take the time to pause and change your mind or assess a situation.

Inner monologue- your inner thoughts, feelings, impulses, and feelings that drive your actions, even as you speak the text.

Your character can be learned

Actors face many challenges. He must first convince his audience that he is the character he portrays. He needs to create convincing illusions to his audience that he is the wizard, the cop or the assassin. It's our job to understand and then wear him on. He must enter in our skin. The character is nothing without us. We bring them alive, and we do it well.

The embodiment of the character. Acting like he

You have done a lot of hard work so far. You have done your research. You have stabilized things in your performance. You have tried many different techniques to help you understand your character. You practice your exercises until you feel everything comes out of your ears. Now comes the magical moment. It's the moment when you are actually the character. The fitting process. Make sure you have everything you need. When you start to wear your clothing, shoes, accessories and other items that are associated with your character, it will become a whole new dimension. Some lines might change dramatically in how you speak them because of the effect that clothes have on actors.

At this stage, actors must realize that they are not the same actor in theory as the character. Even a watch can give a character a unique characteristic. Positive additions to any character include dressing up and trying different looks.

It is also important to consider posture and how you walk. Even if the actors have chosen an outfit that is appropriate for the character, it's possible that something will be different and give the actor a new function. You can accept the change without worrying and you can work around it.

The performances are authentic and natural. The background adds another dimension to the performance, whether it is on stage or on set.

Background

After reading the play or screenplay, we create the background for the character. Then we use the information about the character's past to draw his present life. Even though we don't have sufficient information about his history, we create it for him. This will make his life and existence more solid. An extensive character background gives energy to the character and allows him to participate in the story's action.

The background is a complete CV of the character. From his childhood, we captured him during the actions of the screenplay. We need only certain landmarks. One example is when our character was eight. His parents had an affair and the father split with his wife. He was a graduate when he entered college for a legal degree. At the age 27 he was accused and convicted of harassment. These landmarks can be used to mark the development of a character.

All the middle details. Also, write down everything about their relationship to their family. The screenplay or play will give you all the information. This work will allow the viewer to really get into the characters and become more like them.

Even if you are a bad actor, it doesn't matter if you are a good actor. You should never judge him. Always try to understand and find an explanation for his actions. That will assist you in later stages.

Vision is his vision

Every character on the journey has some objectives to reach during the story. The character is always in a new situation, so the stimulation can be different. This is how you can see it: the character has a challenge to face and overcome. The character must act in a particular way when he is first appearing on stage. This allows us to establish his versatility through the film or play.

Scene Destruction

Breaking down scenes in movies is a difficult task. This has been my practice since before I started studying drama school. My understanding is that I only scratched what else can be done. You have to play around with many things to fully understand the scene's secrets and how actors absorbed them. They then use that information to enlighten you with your performance.